archi-têtes

the id in the grid

First published in Great Britain in 2000 by Wiley-Academy

A division of
JOHN WILEY & SONS
Baffins Lane
Chichester
West Sussex PO19 1UD

ISBN 0-471-98860-X

Copyright © 2000 John Wiley & Sons, Ltd

Other Wiley Editorial Offices
New York • Weinheim • Brisbane • Singapore • Toronto

Designed by Christian Küsters

Printed and bound in Italy

louis hellman

archi-têtes

the id in the grid

WILEY-ACADEMY

contents

= represents importance of the
paragraph, or the words that
are looked in the dictionary

foreword

an obviously true →

One of the basic truisms of architecture is that behind every great
building is a great ego. That fact may be partially obscured by
some ritual incarnation of grand theories or by heartwarming
historical allusions, but it is always there somewhere. Ego, not
argot, is at the heart of architecture.

the process of forming new flesh

Now Louis Hellman, British architect-turned-cartoonist, has come
up with the perfect way of unmasking the id that is invariably at
work within the grid. In a hilarious new series of cartoons he has
drawn several of the world's most famous architects in section
and plan, turning each into an ideal version of his or her personal
architectural style.

the jargon of a group or class.

jargon: words or expression used by a particular group or profession

Contemporary architectural egos as well as historic ones are
fair game for Hellman's pen… 'I think that modern architecture
pretended that design was a matter of analysis and rationalisation',
says Hellman,'which of course it isn't. Architects design according
to a particular personal taste that is a reflection of their own
personalities.'

'That was the idea behind the *Archi-têtes*,' he explains, 'that
architects are the buildings they design. There is also the current
interest in anthropomorphism in architecture, the idea that
buildings are like faces and bodies. They have facades. The whole
vocabulary of architecture is related to the human form and uses
metaphors for the body and for nature. So it was a lot of things
that came together.'

a face of a building.

Peter Lemos, *Metropolis*, May 1985

the attribution of a human form or personality to a god, animal or a thing.

6

every man's work,
whether it be literature
or music or architecture
or anything else,
is always a portrait
of himself.

samuel butler, 'the way of all flesh', 1903

introduction

The *Archi-têtes* series was actually conceived in 1984 as an
entry to a cartoon competition held by the *Architectural Review*.
Bearing in mind the international readership of the magazine,
I wanted a format that did not need captions and that would
have global appeal. The germ of the idea came to me in a
dentist's waiting room and I doodled a rough version of Le
Corbusier as one of his plans on the proverbial back of an
envelope. Was it possible to do caricatures of famous
architects using elements of their buildings? Next I roughed
out Frank Lloyd Wright, Mies and Norman Foster. It seemed to
work, if I worked at it. I completed ten or so, including Aalto,
Stirling, Venturi, a later Corb and Voysey. I won the competition
and the caricatures were published in the *Review* (except
Voysey, which the Editor did not like). More followed on and
off but not on a regular basis.

  Where precisely the inspiration came from I do not know.
The most celebrated historical pedigree for the idea of
portraits composed of natural or man-made elements can be
found in the work of the sixteenth-century Mannerist painter
Arcimboldo whose simulacra, composed of flowers, fruit or
meat, influenced the Surrealists like Dalí and Ernst. However
in terms of an attempt at caricaturing the famous using
their own products, I think the *Archi-têtes* are fairly unique.

Louis Hellman

[handwritten annotation:] of a specific characteristic

[handwritten annotation:] an image of something, a shadowy likeness.

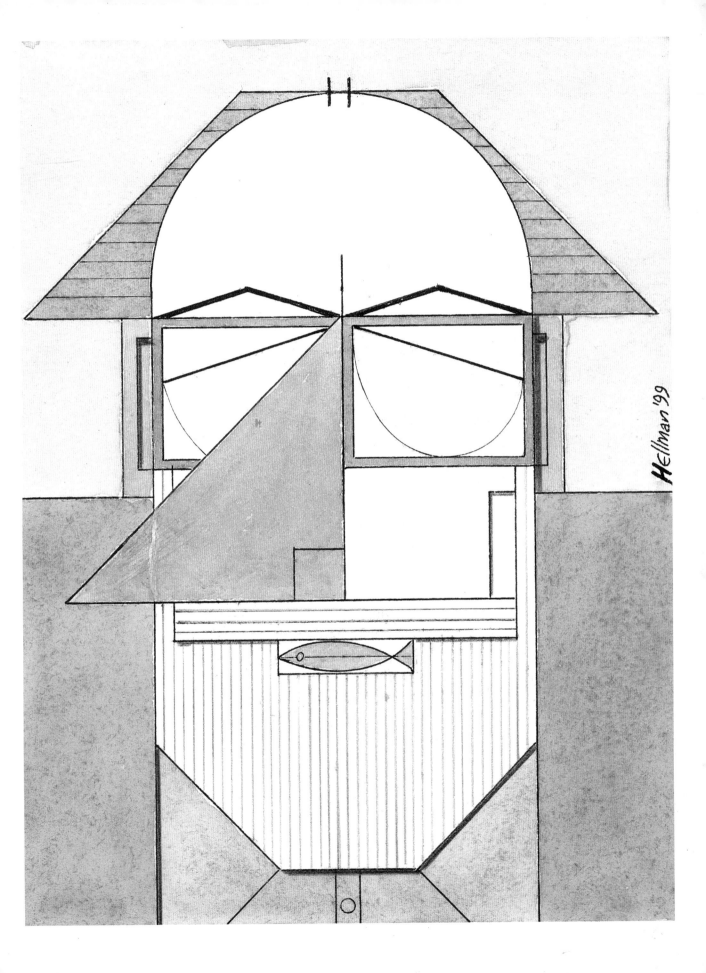

Hellman '99

3

2

alvar aalto

1

**alvar aalto did not say much,
no cant, jargon or double dutch,
but his surfaces never diminish,
they are what you might call 'double finnish'.**

The great Finnish architect Alvar Aalto (1898–1976), like Sibelius in music, drew on national landscape and architecture, especially the traditional Karelian farmhouse, to develop a humane form of Modernism. He often employed 'old' materials such as brick, tile, stone, wood or copper in new forms with new production techniques. Prior to this' he had designed in the Modernist or Constructivist white mode but always with great flair, imagination and concern for people. The turning point came with the Villa Mairea (1938) which integrated tradition and Modernism without compromising either. Aalto's lack of arcane dogma and his recognition of tradition marginalised him for a time after the war, during the hegemony of hard line Modernism, but he is now recognised as a leading pioneer and a prophet of the current emphasis on formal complexity and symbolism.

Normally the older a subject the more material there is for caricature in the form of lines, bags, double chins and so on. However, this *Archi-tête* is a portrait of Aalto in early middle age, based on his organically-derived plan forms. The ear is a typical fan shape, much favoured by Aalto, while the hair relates to his uniquely inventive use of curved, laminated hardwood in furniture and interiors. The Finnish landscape of lakes and forests is also hinted at. It is no secret that, like so many dour and doomy Finns, Aalto was a hard drinker and this aspect is apparent in the drawing. Caricature is rarely kind.

Stage 1
1. Preliminary caricature from photographs

Stage 2
Study of building plans and architectural photographs
2. Finnish Pavilion, New York Fair

Stage 3
3. First freehand sketch

Hellman

1

2

3

will
alsop

does will alsop say,
when down in marseilles,
'merci et grace a dieu,
pour le grand sacré bleu'?

▷ *independant minded person*

Will Alsop (1947), a Northampton-born architect/artist, represents the loose cannon of contemporary British architecture. He is unclassifyable, except as a sort of maverick neo-Expressionist Deconstructivist. A product of the late 1960s Alsop trained at the AA under Peter Cook, worked for Cedric Price and taught sculpture at St Martin's School of Art before forming a partnership first with John Lyall and then with the German Jan Störmer in 1990. A self-styled avant-garde architect, Alsop maintains he works out his designs by means of large-scale paintings in the manner of Howard Hodgkin accepting that building design is not a matter of form-follows-function analysis but is irrational and intuitive. All this is good PR posturing stuff to shock old Modernists. However, Alsop's first major building, the Hôtel

du Département (1994) local authority HQ in Marseilles (*Le Grand Bleu* to locals), despite its bizarre, ultramarine, steel-clad, zoomorphic forms, is as highly functional and elementally articulated as any Modern Movement creation, even down to its *post hoc* style justification of being streamlined against the harsh Mistral and Sirocco winds. Like any modern architect Alsop claims that architecture should be above style. Yet he seems to have abandoned the quirky originality of Marseilles for the current fashion of globulous Deconstructivism, employing stylistic devices like the 'potty pilotis' on his Peckham Library cribbed from Rem Koolhaas.

Alsop's appearance is increasingly fleshily porcine, a sort of bloated John Sessions. The *Archi-tête* presents him, when he still had long hair, as a version of *Le Grand Bleu*.

▷ *og or like pigs.*

Stage 1
1. Preliminary caricature from photographs

Stage 2
Study of building plans and architectural photographs
2. Le Grand Bleu, Marseilles

Stage 3
3. First freehand sketch

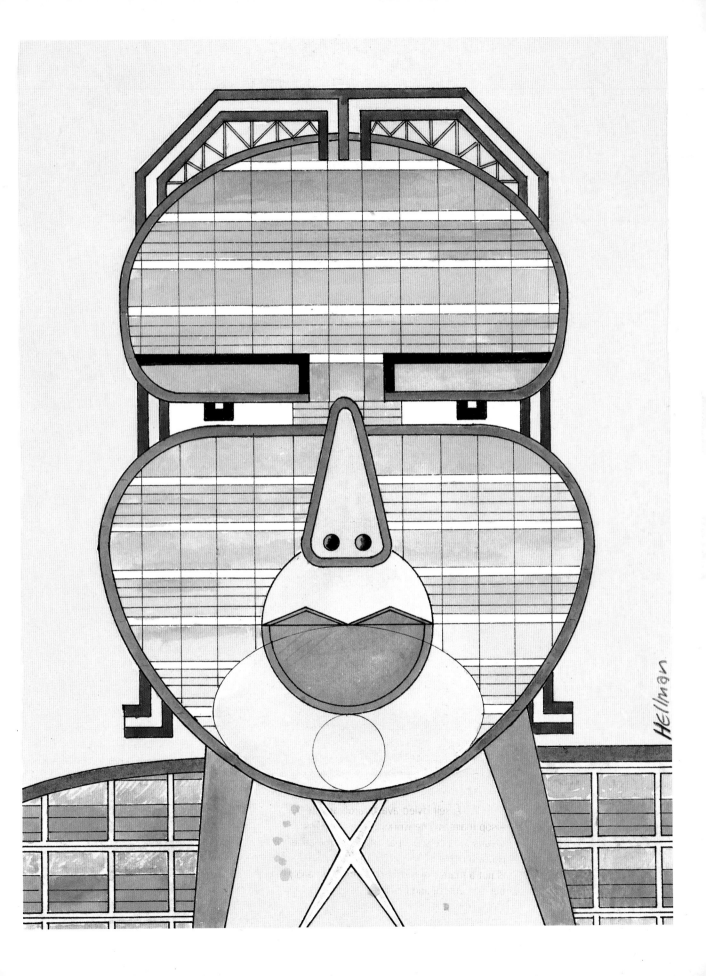

Hellman

1

2

tadao
ando

3

ando,
land low,
sky high,
walls tie.

orientation; a person's attitude or adjusment in relation to circumstances, esp politically or psychologically.

unchangeable always the same

relating to monastery

Tadao Ando (1941), self-taught and based in Osaka, is the most influential of the Post-Modern, second-generation Japanese architects. Although labelled as 'Minimalist' Ando's prime concern is to integrate modern form and traditional Japanese conceptual devices such as *shakkei* (building as 'borrowed scenery'), and *oku.* (where 'the artificial is mystically integrated into the surrounding natural environment'), not to 'commune with nature as it is but rather to change the meaning of nature through architecture'. Ando claims his materials are raw concrete, sun, sky, shadow and water, in other words: space. His insistence that his clients experience nature led him in one early house to separate the living and sleeping areas by an open court. His buildings, both domestic and public, are beautifully crafted, spiritual or even monastic experiences invariably using untreated concrete internally and externally. To Western eyes they might be thought to verge on the pretentious or precious, there is no room for the clutter that characterises homes here, people do not generally live like monks especially if children are around. There is a current fashion in some quarters for Minimalism and Japanese mystical orientations such as *feng shui*, but it invariably smacks of astrology or middle-class posturing.

crowded and untidy collection of things

Ando seems always to have had a 'mop-head' appearance and the *Archi-tête* refers to this, presenting him as one of his cool axonometrics where the building reaches out to the surrounding landscape.

Stage 1
1. Preliminary caricature from photographs

Stage 2
Study of building plans and architectural photographs
2. Water Temple

Stage 3
3. First freehand sketch

2

3.1

1

mario botta

3.2

mario botta
has built a lotta
romanesque pomo
well north of como.

fortified: provide or equip with defensive works so as to strengthen against attack.

sprawl: sit or lie or fall with limbs flung out

useful

Mario Botta (1943), the Swiss-Italian Neo-Rationalist, studied in Venice under Carlo Scarpa and worked for Le Corbusier and Louis Kahn. He was a leading member of the Ticinese School which sought to combine Italian Neo-Rationalism with local regional tradition, a typically Swiss approach which maintains the *canton* while absorbing outside influences. Botta's rural houses utilise strong geometric primary forms such as cubes or cylinders constructed in concrete block, out of which are carved apertures for windows or doors to frame views of the landscape. They claim to be both modern and traditional, using up-to-date technology while evoking agricultural buildings such as barns or silos, as well as regional tower houses and Roman architecture. Yet there is something ironic in the wealthy Swiss middle classes commissioning these crafted and fortified towers while the 'peasants' live in the usual suburban sprawl. Inevitably Botta has transferred and inflated this house form when designing commercial urban buildings such as banks. The results are none too successful.

Botta's appearance is very much like one of his geometric houses: round face, round eyes, round glasses all framed in a mass of thick curls (vegetation). The *Archi-tête* has him as one of his cut-away bird's-eye axonometrics, although he has come out looking rather oriental.

Da pit or air tight structure in which green crops are pressed and kept for fodder

a dried hay or straw.

2

iakov
chernikhov

3.1

3.2

1

**joe stalin said to chernikhov,
'stop that fantasy, turn it off,
your predictions i can't abide,
the future is what i decide!'**

Stage 1
1. Preliminary caricature from photographs

Stage 2
Study of building plans and architectural photographs
2. Composition from Construction of Architectural and Machine Forms, 1931

Stage 3
3.1 & 3.2. First freehand sketches

Iakov Chernikhov (1889–1951), like Sant'Elia and Archigram, has exerted considerable influence by means of futuristic graphic renderings without the inconvenience of having to attempt to build them. A working class hero and loner, Chernikhov worked his way through college in Odessa and Leningrad to graduate as an 'architect artist' in 1925. Complementing the post-revolution Moscow Constructivist school led by Melnikov, Ginsburg and the Vesnin brothers, Chernikhov published a series of books in Leningrad on Constructivist theory illustrated by 'architectural fantasies' or 'fictions' celebrating industrialism, machine production and the 'scientific city'. These articulated, dynamic and expressive drawings (worked on by student admirers) represent a kind of marriage of Suprematism and mechanical engineering, a romantic Constructivist vision in contrast to the more mathematical, rationalist approach of the Moscow group.

However, by the 1930s, Stalins dictatorship clamped down on all forms of 'progressive' art. The officially approved style of

Architecture became the oppressive, over-blown stripped-Classical monumentalism beloved of most totalitarian regimes. Chernikhov's books were banned and he was prevented from teaching or practising, although he continued to produce fantasy projects. He was 'discovered' in the late 1980s, along with the other Constructivists, as part of the general Post-Modern plundering of the history of modern-architecture for 'new ideas', like fashionable Deconstructivism. Such architectural fantasies have their place in the development of the art, but they have their dangers as well. They tend to represent architecture as purely a matter of style or expression, and conveniently omit its other requirements for utility, function, context and practicality, which is why they are so rife in schools of architecture.

Photographs of Chernikhov show him as a somewhat suave Slav, with high cheekbones, long nose, deep-set eyes and sensuous mouth. The *Archi-tête* portrays him as one of his red black and blue Constructivist renderings, distinctly robotic.

18

Hellman

1

2

r. buckminster fuller had verve,
his genius we did not deserve,
he tried to make homes,
out of geodesic domes,
but you can't fit a bed in a curve.

richard buckminster

fuller

*Geodesic: of or relation to
geodesy.
Geodesic line: the shortest
possible line between
two points on a curved
surface.
Geodesy: the branch of
mathematics dealing with the
figures and areas of the earth*

*17
8 7 13
1983
- 1895
88*

88 yrs

*bring about by
incitement or
persuasion; provoke*

*a long
upright
post
of
timber.*

Stage 1
1. Preliminary caricature from
photographs

Stage 2
Study of building plans and
architectural photographs
2. American Society of Metals

Stage 3
3. First freehand sketch

Richard Buckminster Fuller (1895–1983) was
a twentieth-century *uomo universale*: an
architect, engineer, mathematician,
environmentalist, inventor, visionary,
philosopher, guru, marathon orator and
so on. He instigated the *portmanteau* or
technology transfer school of super
functionalist design with the Dymaxion
(dynamic + maximum efficiency) House
(1927), which was mass produced using
car or plane technology and suspended
from a service core mast. Then there were
Tensegrity (tension + integrity) structures,
or 'space frames', composed of tension
rods joined by components in compression.
However, his most famous invention is the
Geodesic Dome which uses small, standard
components, clipped together in tetrahedral
or octahedral units, to enclose the maximum
space related to surface area. This dome
could be made from any material and in any
size, from a hut to a lid forManhattan, and

could be dropped by helicopter.
Marginalised as a nut by architects,
Fuller came into his own in the 1960s.
This was the age of space travel, youth
culture, ecological awareness. Every
hippie commune had a geodesic dome
made of junk and Fuller's Planet Earth,
World Design Concept was a hit. He has
since had a huge influence on High-Tech
architects with their light-but-strong
structures ('More with less', to paraphrase
Mies) and their obsession with homes
mass produced like cars.
Bucky looked like Eisenhower crossed
with Michelin Man: bald, domed head,
thick-rimmed glasses, visionary gaze,
button nose and wide mouth. The *Archi-
tête* has a typical geodesic dome dropped
by helicopter for the head, the Dymaxion
House for the face, the world view for
eyes and his Dymaxion World Map for bow
tie. Eat your heart out *Time Magazine*.

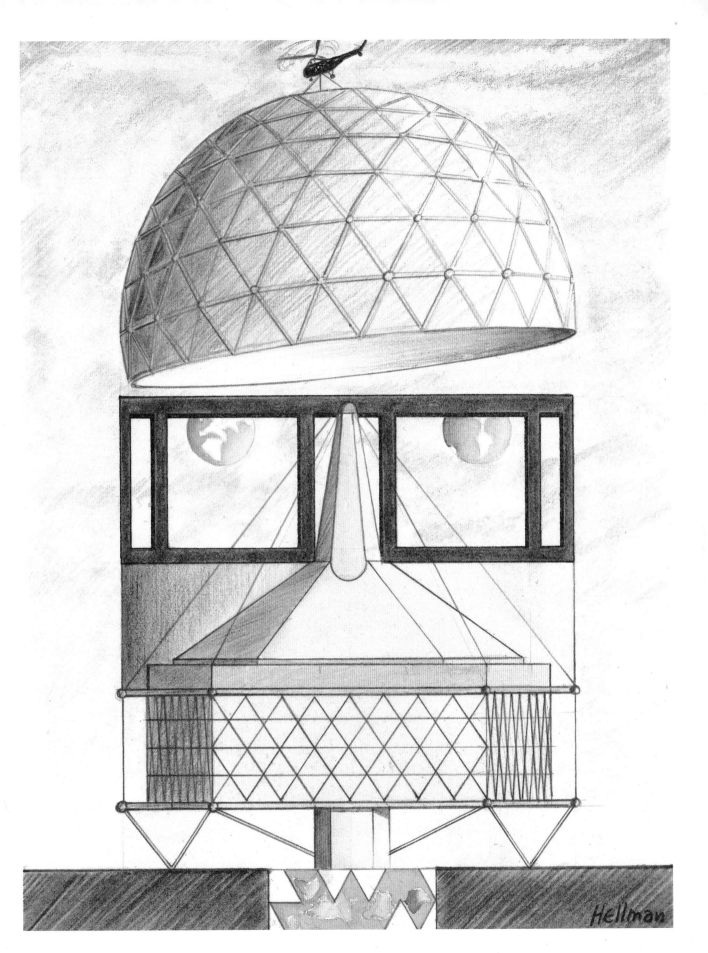

Hellman

3

1

coop himmelblau

2

that dutch museum by coop himmelblau was built by groninger ship builders, you know, dynamic forms rise and fall, now here, now there, er, excuse me, i've a touch of mal de mer.

Wolf Prix (1942) and Helmut Swiczinsky (1944), Vienna-based *enfants terribles*, formed Coop Himmelblau in 1968 designing pneumatic projects. Under the influence of Hollein and Domenig, they turned to an architecture which reacted to the sloppiness of Post-Modernism and which was uncomfortable, disturbing and shocking. They wanted an architecture that 'bleeds, which exhausts, which revolves and breaks . . . which shines, which stings, shreds and splits apart while revolving. Architecture must burn. An architecture of the chest spiked by the steering column.' This rather quaint neo-Futurist rhetoric resulted in images with a lot of spikey bits penetrating solid bits, and one or two bar interiors. There was also an aim to evolve buildings which were literally anthropomorphic and would 'breathe' and change in response to the user's needs.

However like the Modernists and Functionalism, Coop Himmelblau's built examples comprise static *images* of organic metamorphosis, spine and wing forms, like the extension on the roof of the Ronacher Theatre (1987). Now not so *enfant* or *terrible*, they have won major commissions like the museum at Groningen, a rather perfunctory exercise in fashionable Deconstructivism, which they pioneered, supposedly, using ship-building technology.

Prix and Swiczinsky are the typical double act: the thin one with the glasses and the rotund one with the comic moustache, Warhol and Walensa, Holly and Hussein, George and Grass. The *Archi-tête* has them as a version of Groningen reflected in the river with heavenly blue sky, naturally, and spikey truss forms as hair, glasses and moustache. Crazy name, crazy guys (they'd like to think).

Stage 1
1. Preliminary caricatures from photographs

Stage 2
Study of building plans and architectural photographs
2. Museum at Groningen

Stage 3
3. First freehand sketch

Hellman

sear: scorch, esp. with a hot iron; cauterize, brand.

latterly: in the latter part of life or of a period.

2

3.1

pterodactyl: a large extinct flying bird like reptile with a long slender head and neck.

prominent: jutting out; projecting 2. conspicuous. 3. distinguished; important.

clearly visible

günther

domenig

semtex: odourless plastic explosive

3.2

i went to the z bank,
but when there my heart sank,
to find i had paid a
cheque in to darth vader.

▷ *the state of being prominent.*

▷ *of quiet and steady character*

Günther Domenig (1934) is the leading figure of the anarchic, neo-Expressionist Granz school in south-east Austria and professor of the Technical University there. He first came to prominence with the Z Bank on the Vienna Favoriten (1979), which introduced his sculptural, subversive, suggestive style (Scharoun on speed) into the staid capital. The upper, metallic street elevation of the savings bank, like a 1950s car radiator grille or *Star Wars* helmet, suddenly collapses at the lower storey as if hit by a semtex blast. A comment on the fluctuations of the financial markets perhaps? The interior is even weirder, a riot of stainless steel ductwork tentacles, searing fluorescent lights and a huge hand 'of some mythic giant as if he is trying to grope his way out of the bowels of the building' to secure a loan perhaps? Domenig's subsequent architecture is sensual, multi-directional, anti-intellectual and latterly classified as Deconstructivist, which he would no doubt deny. 'I would prefer it if architectural critics and art historians just wrote poems about my work,' he has said, although he probably did not mean comic verses.

Domenig in middle age bears some resemblance to the lived-in features of Lee Marvin, 'I was born under a decon star'? The folded facade of the Z Bank transfers well in this *Archi-tête*, with one of Domenig's pterodactylic birds on his shoulder.

Stage 1
1. Preliminary caricature from photographs

seeking to subvert.

Stage 2
Study of building plans and architectural photographs
2. Starter Complex

overturn, overthrow

Stage 3
3.1 & 3.2 First freehand sketches

24

2

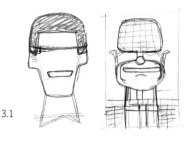

3.1

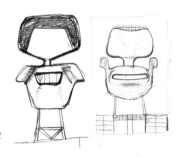

3.2

1

the
eames

our old lounge chair made by the eames
is falling apart at the seams,
we used to muse while we'd swivel,
now we just creak and speak drivel,
and wallow in flared sixties dreams.

Stage 1
1. Preliminary caricature from
photographs

Stage 2
Study of building plans and
architectural photographs
2. DCW chairs

Stage 3
3.1 & 3.2 First freehand sketches

76yrs
Ray (1912–88) and Charles Eames
61yrs (1907–78) were pioneering Californian
designers. They had a huge influence on
all aspects of design, including architecture,
furniture, products, toys, exhibitions and film,
predating the universal designers of the
1980s like Starck or Arad. Artist Ray and
architect Charles, partners in life and work,
complemented each other and unlocked
each other's potential. Individually they were
average, together they achieved greatness.
'They were a compound, not a mixture.' In
1949, they designed their house and studio
in Pacific Palisades made of standardised,
mass-produced components which had a
great impact on the architectural world.
It was cool, laid-back, anti-rhetorical and had
a delicate Japanese feel.

They developed a range of affordable,
mass-produced, high-quality furniture using
glass-fibre, plywood and wire construction,

as well as the more up-market study chair
and ottoman which is now a classic. They
pioneered exhibition and film communications
techniques for government and corporate
big business. The Eames combined populism
and cultured intellectualism, the art of the
ordinary and the application of modern
science and technology, as well as mass
production and American individualism.

Charles had that clean-cut, Californian,
bow-tied, look much like a William Holden
1950s screen idol. The *Archi-tête* has him
as a moulded plywood and wire chair, with
the Eames house as his jacket and bow-tie.
Although equal partners, in typical 1950s
and 1960s chauvinist fashion, Charles got
most of the credit, or took it. The balance
has been redressed a little with a chairperson
version of Ray, who had the appearance of a
wholesome but strong American pioneering
woman. Mainstreames?

26

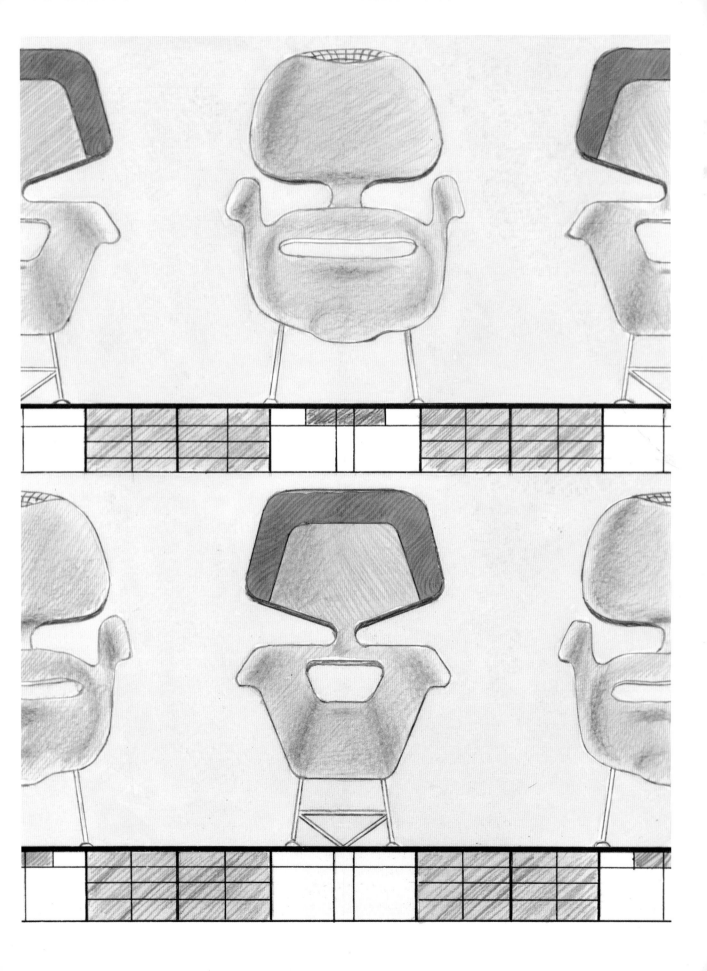

2

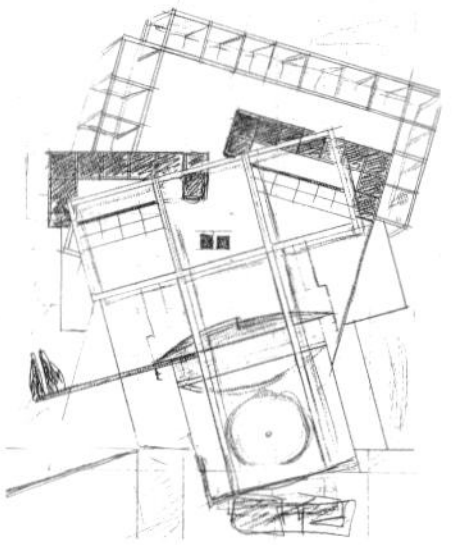

3

cemantic: relating to meanings in language.
neologism: a new word or expression

peter
eisenman

terragni and eisenman coming,
so i guess i'm gonna go,
mumbo-jumbo and pomo punning,
non-building in ohio.

(with apologies to csny)

oblique: not going straight to the point.

obscure or confuse

Stage 1
1. Preliminary caricature from photographs

Stage 2
Study of building plans and architectural photographs
2. Extension to Ohio State University

Stage 3
3. First freehand sketch

Peter Eisenman (1932) is another American Post-Modernist whose career was boosted as a member of the famous New York Five in 1972, although borrowing from Italian Neo-Realism and Terragni's fascist white Modernism rather than Le Corbusier. Eisenman designed several houses, pretentiously calling them House I, II, III and so on, as if they were abstract paintings, and took architectural theorising to new heights of semantic neologistic obfuscation. To quote Tom Wolfe, his 'great genius was to use relatively clear words from the linguistic lingo and lead one's poor brain into the Halusian Gulp.' Eisenman aimed at something called 'autonomous architecture' and the 'non-building', exemplified in House VI where

a non-staircase leads to a non-upper floor. He beat other PoMos, when he won the competition for the Wexner Center for experimental art at Ohio State University, Columbus (1983–89). Here two decorative gridded non-structures slice through the existing campus at oblique angles fronted by deconstructed toy-town castle forms paying ironic reference to the demolished mock medieval Armory building. Total self indulgence but the university was willing to cough up for this expensive folly.

Eisenman resembles a smug 1950s professor or journalist, as played by Steve Martin: specs, pipe, bow-tie, braces. The *Archi-tête* deconstructs him in Wexner plan fashion, with the Noddy castles as pipe and bow-tie.

showing self government.
acting independently or having the freedom to do so.

28

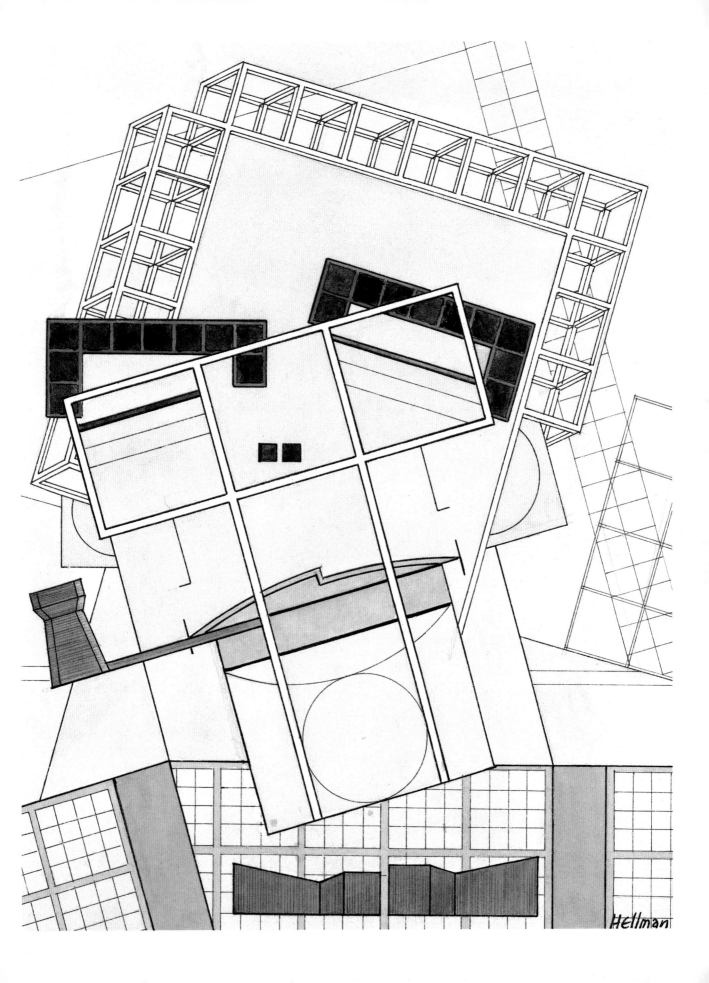

Hellman

1

2

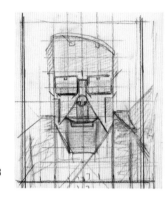

3

ralph
erskine

byker, byker art thou fine,
by the waters o' the tyne?
i don't know, perhaps it fails,
go and ask the prince of wales.

monolith : a single block of stone, esp. shaped into a pillar or monument.

relating to this architect

Stage 1
1. Preliminary caricature from photographs

Stage 2
Study of building plans and architectural photographs
2. Library in Stockholm

Stage 3
3. First freehand sketch

Ralph Erskine (1914) pioneered a form of community architecture with an approach influenced by Team X and Alvar Aalto, which combined regional tradition with modern technology. In 1939, he left England for Sweden where he participated in its post-war social idealism and regeneration through modern architecture, often designing for northern Arctic sites where buildings have to cope with extreme climates. Erskine's ideal of user participation was exercised most famously in the Byker social housing scheme of 1969–80 in Newcastle, which rehoused 80 per cent of a community of ten thousand living in an area of back-to-back 'slums'. Erskine set up an office on the site, where tenants could come to consult with the architects on the plan forms of their flats, on who their neighbours would be and on detailed design. Although this was a great advance on the old autocratic architectural approach, particularly for the enclosed

an absolute ruler

traditional houses, the resulting long, monolithic barrier block, varying in height, texture and colour, and incorporating Erskine's garden-shed vernacular, showed that the architect was very much in control. It represents the last of the megastructure monuments to the housing 'problem', with the attendant technical problems. From the 1980s Erskine architecture has taken on some Post-Modern aspects, such as the Stockholm University Library and the notorious Ark office block in London.

In appearance, Erskine might be a rather earnest liberal headmaster or veteran jazz musician. The *Archi-tête* combines Stockholm Library elements for the head, nose and mouth with Byker balconies for the eyes and glasses. The jacket, shirt and tie are formed by elevations of the wall with its bands of different coloured brickwork. Somehow, it bears an unfortunate and unintended resemblance to John Major.

30

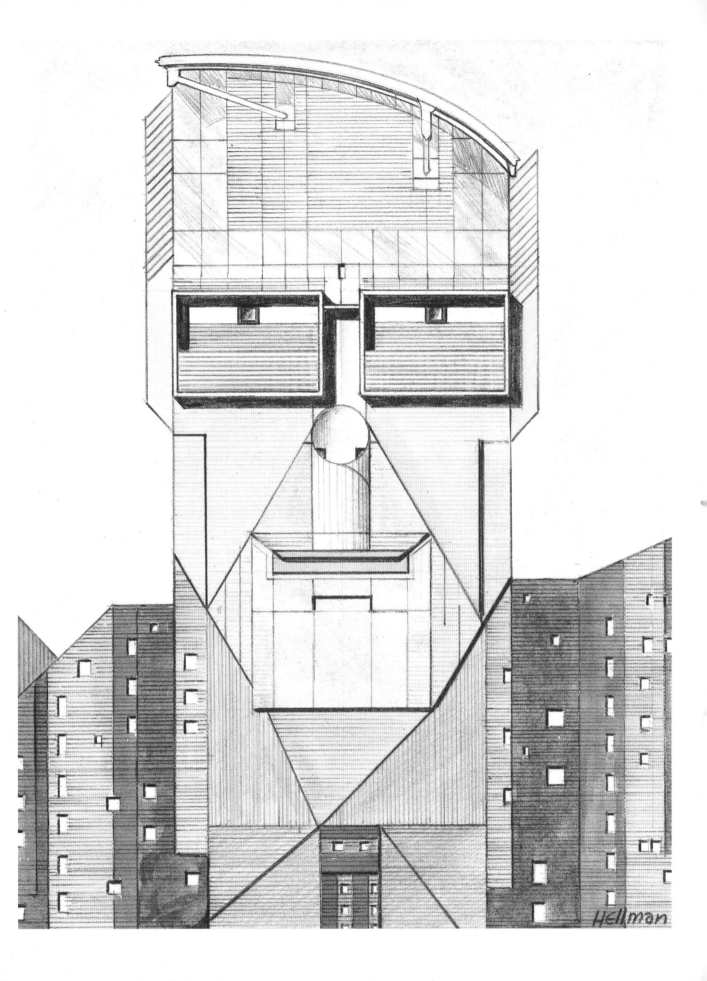

Hellman

2

1

3.1

terry
farrell

3.2

terry fowl at tvam,
laid some eggs and caused mayhem,
said he, 'the yoke's not over yet,
wait 'till you see my oeufs complets!'

Stage 1
1. Preliminary caricature from photographs

Stage 2
Study of building plans and architectural photographs
2. Television studios in Camden Town, London

Stage 3
3.1 & 3.2 First freehand sketches

Terry Farrell (1938) became Britain's *Numero Uno* PoMo after his 1980 divorce from his equally famous partner Nicholas Grimshaw. The latter continued the practice's High-Tech approach, while Farrell saw the leitmotiv and went eclectic Post-Modern under the influence of Americans like Graves and Moore, Art Deco, Otto Wagner and anything else you can think of. He first hit the headlines with his TVAM Breakfast Television HQ (1983), a converted car workshop in Camden town, with its eggs-in-cups cod urns pun-ctuating the roof line. Since then, he has built prodigiously with commercial blocks around the UK and in the City of London, using a variety of styles including PoMo, Mock Classical and Dec-tech, most notoriously with his High Az-tech wedding cake HQ for M16 on the Thames. He has now gone global in places as far flung as Hong Kong and Edinburgh.

Terry Farrell has always had a somewhat Neanderthal mien: bushy eyebrows, deep-set eyes, small nose, thick lips making him a good subject for caricature. The *Archi-tête* shows him at the start of his PoMotion as a version of the TVAM building with its piped string courses, tubular keystone cop out and metal cladding. The eyebrows are a version of his Covent Garden, flower shop, joke glass impediments.

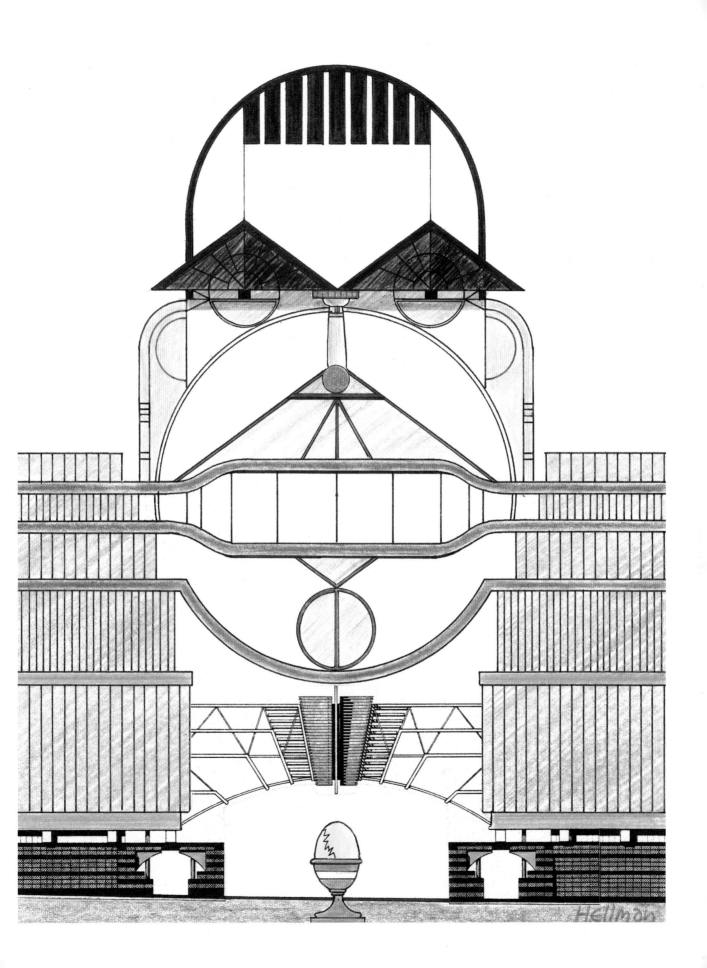

Hellman

2

1

hassan
fathy

3

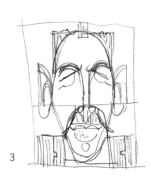

hassan fathy,
threw a party,
dress informal,
bring a camel.

*vernacular: the language or
dialect of a particular
country.*

impose: require

lofty: imposing height

Stage 1
1. Preliminary caricature from
photographs

Stage 2
Study of building plans and
architectural photographs.
2. Gouache by Fathy

Stage 3
3. First freehand sketch

89 yrs

Hassan Fathy (1900–89), Egyptian architect-philosopher, was practising vernacular 'community architecture' as an alternative to dogmatic Modernism about fifty years before Prince Charles 'discovered' it. Fathy organised housing in rural Egypt using four thousand-year-old traditional building methods, such as sun-baked bricks, and employing local, unskilled labour. He claimed that this was superior economically, ecologically, socially and politically to the bland, energy-guzzling Modernist blocks advocated by most architects and imposed by neo-colonialist Western capitalism. Fathy believed traditional architecture had 'evolved its own favourite forms, as peculiar to the people as its language, its dress, its folklaw… and the

buildings of any locality were the beautiful children of a happy marriage between the imagination of the people and the demands of the countryside.' Whether the poor accepted these lofty Morrisonian ideals is not clear. Fathy saw tradition and continuity as important in creating a humane environment and was consequently ignored by the architectural historical establishment until the 1970s.

The aged Fathy had a fine face to caricature: moustache, large ears, domed head and a slightly raffish air. The *Archi-tête* portrays him as one of his sensitive gouache architectural representations which also eschews Western Modernist, single-perspective renderings of buildings, people and landscape.

avoid.

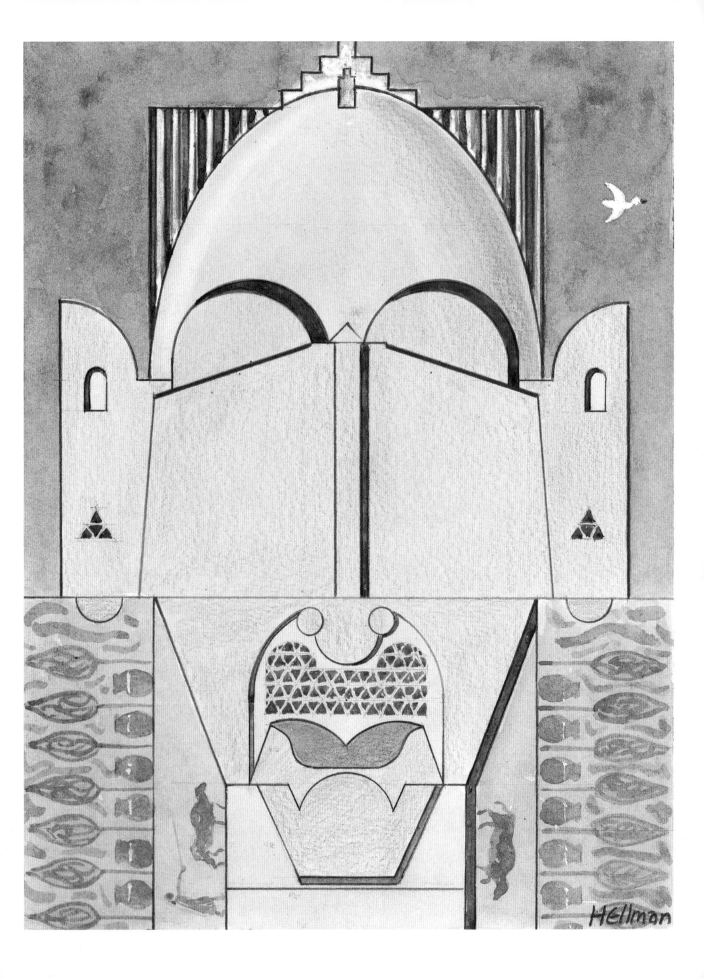

Hellman

2

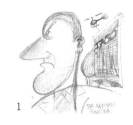

1

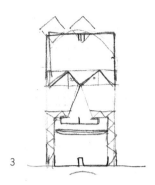

3

norman
foster

atrium: the central court of an ancient Roman house. skylit central court rising through several storeys with galleries and rooms opening off at each level.

drab: small scattered amount.

orthogonal: of or involving right angles.

truss: a framework.

norman foster, king of high-tech, has tubular steel for a neck, a pity his brain can't be seen, it's made entirely of neoprene!

> producing many offspring or much output.

satanic: diabolical, hellish

Norman Foster (1935) is the most prolific and successful British architect ever. He has evolved an internationally applicable brand of High-Tech architecture, originally based on open-plan highly serviced 'flexible' sheds, exposed steel structures and thin external skin cladding. Born of working-class Manchester parents, Foster left school at sixteen and became interested in architecture while working as a clerk in Waterhouse's Manchester Town Hall. After national service in the RAF, he worked his way through architecture school and won a scholarship to Yale where he met Richard Rogers and was exposed to the influence of Paul Rudolph, Buckminster Fuller, the Eames, SOM and Mies. Other European mentors were Paxton, Prouvé and Max Bill's Bauhaus notions of *Produktform* or buildings conceived as anonymous containers using technology transfer principles from aeroplanes or industrial design. In 1971, Foster set up his own practice, achieving fame with the Willis Faber Dumas Headquarters (1975) for a firm of Ipswich insurance brokers. Dubbed the 'grand piano' by locals, the external reflective glass curtain wall follows the curved site boundary providing a two-storey *bürolandschaft* (open-plan offices around a central atrium containing escalators), a staff swimming pool and roof garden. Recently listed, the building excited architects in the way it reflected and deconstructed its drab surroundings, demonstrating that Modernism was not confined to orthogonal boxiness. After the Sainsbury 'aircraft hanger' gallery at the University of East Anglia, Norwich (1978), Foster's practice took off with the Hong Kong and Shanghai Bank (1979), the most expensive building in the world at the time, with its massive external trusses, vast atrium and (little-used) computer-controlled sun reflector. With it, Foster perfected the building as corporate brand image and the bank's construction personified multi-national capitalism, combining cheap labour and advanced technology.

Now virtually bald with a prominent nose, large jaw and slightly satanic eyes, Foster resembles the villain from a 1930s sci-fi film. The first *Archi-tête*, c1985, forms the head from the Gropius-style Thamesmead Art Glass Factory and the nose from the Honkers Shankers 'ladder' columns. The chin is a version of the Sainsbury facade and the jacket is based on Ipswich reflections.

Stage 1
1. Preliminary caricature from photographs

Stage 2
Study of building plans and architectural photographs
2. Renault Distribution Centre, Swindon

Stage 3
3. First freehand sketch

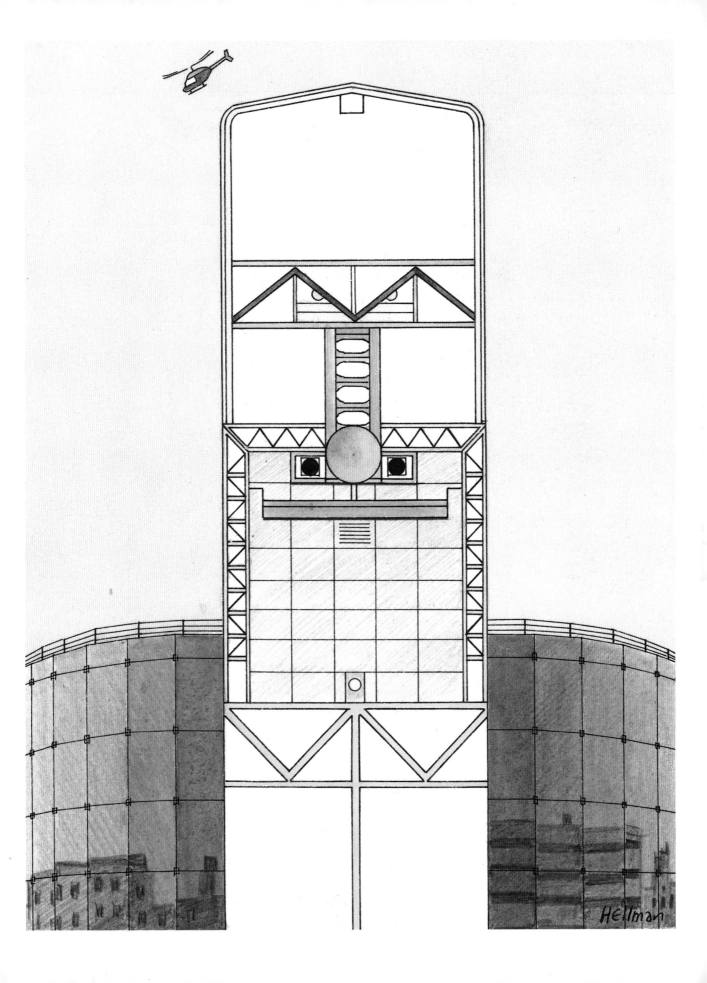

Hellman

1

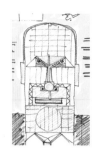

3

2

lord
foster

peerage; peers as a class; the nobility. 2. the rank of peer or peeress.

serried: pressed together, without gap.

abrasive: harsh

pseudo - (1) supposed or purporting to be but not really so.

foster's a knight,
the queen did right,
she knew the form,
'high rise, sir norm!'

*risibly :(risible, (1) laughable, ludicrous.)
(2) Inclined to laugh.*

Stage 1
1. Preliminary caricature from photographs

Stage 2
Study of building plans and architectural photographs
2. Hong Kong & Shanghai Bank

Stage 3
3. First freehand sketch

Following the success and prestige of the Hong Kong and Shanghai Bank, Foster's international fame and work load expanded rapidly with major commissions for banks, airports, museums, assemblies, office blocks, stations, bridges and urban designs in Britain, Europe and the Far East. Only the US seems to have escaped his net. He has received every architectural gong and honour going, and was knighted in 1990, followed by the OM in 1998 and a peerage in 1999. Foster operates from a purpose-built London HQ (with private pent-house above), where some five hundred young cosmopolitan Foster clones in serried ranks are overseen by the leader. He is now a multi-millionaire, owning his own helicopter and jet which he pilots himself. An abrasive, energetic and widelyknowledgeable character, Sir Norman ('Stormin' Norman some call him) is master of the architect's pseudo-rational justification for the rightness of his own solutions and it is clear why clients flock to him. Foster prides himself on his lateral approach and it is said

that early on he advised one client that rather than building, his problem would be better solved by leaving his wife. An all-jogging, all-skiing fitness freak, Foster still believes in the old Modernist apolitical technology transfer principle of design, rather risibly citing the Boeing 747 as his favourite 'building'. However, since the insertion of the Sackler galleries above the Royal Academy in London, Foster has even tackled the adaptation and modernisation of historic buildings with flair and imagination, notably at the British Museum and the Reichstag in Berlin.

The second *Archi-tête*, a cover commissioned by the now defunct *Progressive Architecture* magazine, has a version of the Reichstag glass dome as head, a Renault factory stanchion and Wessex school for nose and eyebrows, the Sainsbury Arts Centre again as cheeks, the Valencia Congress and Techno HQ for ears, the Aksa table design for Techno as chin, the Duxford Aircraft Museum for neck, Stansted Airport as tie and the Fréjus Regional School forms the body.

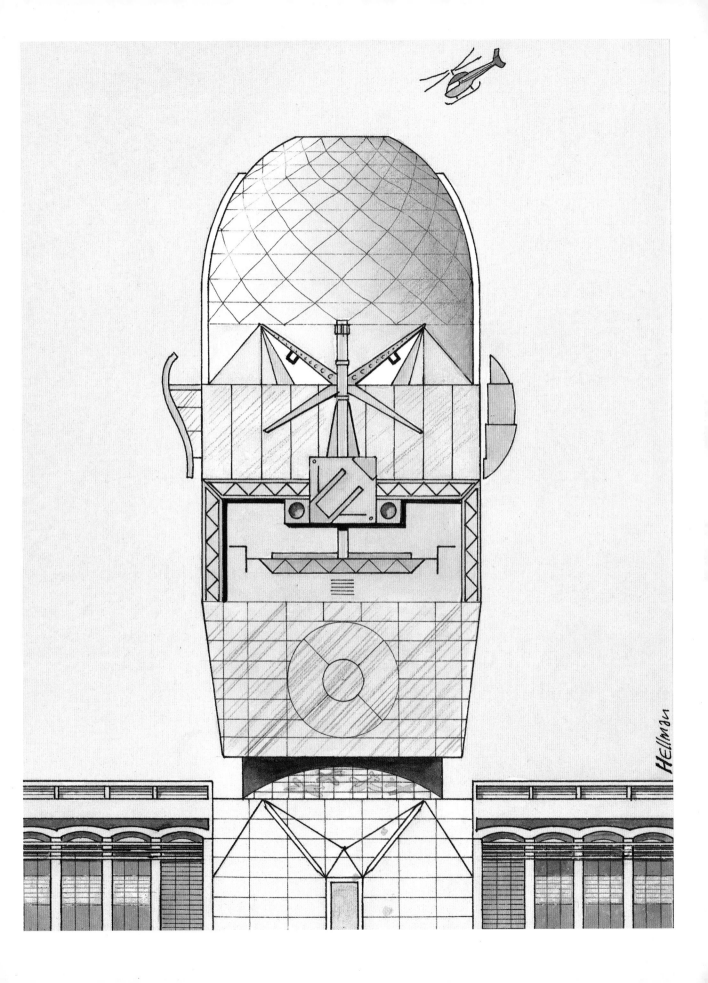

1

3.1

2

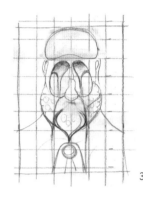

3.2

antonio
gaudí

gaudí, like catalan vines,
thrived where the curve intertwines,
but technology won,
when he died in the sun,
killed by a tram on straight lines.

Antoni Gaudí (1852–1926), the great Catalan maverick, was described by Pevsner in 1952 as 'the only genius produced by the Art Nouveau'. However, it is now clear that the label 'Art Nouveau' is far too restricting to categorise Gaudí's work, which encompassed Spanish Gothic, Symbolism, Surrealism, structural innovation and organic architecture, as exemplified in his masterpieces in Barcelona: the Sagrada Familia, the Casa Batlló, the Casa Milà and the Parc Güell. Gaudí asserted that the straight line belonged to man and the curve to God, and his formal and structural inspiration was drawn from organic elements such as bones, muscles, wings, shells, plants and caves as well as clouds, waves or stars. He might even be seen as a precursor of late twentieth-century Deconstructivism. At best, Gaudí's buildings and interiors have a dynamic, fluid quality, although there is also sometimes a Disney-like kitsch. When he was fatally hit by a tram in Barcelona, nobody recognised the shabby old man but thousands attended his funeral. In 1998, there was a move to have Gaudí canonised.

The aged Gaudí bore some resemblance to an old Catalan sea captain: deep-set eyes, weatherbeaten skin, white beard and cropped white hair. The anthropomorphic nature of the Casa Batlló inspired this *Archi-tête*, with its bone-like structure (head and beard), mask or skull-shaped balconies (cheeks) and scaly dragon roof (coat). The shirt is based on a typical Gaudí stained-glass window or ceramic tile, and the tie is a finial from the Sagrada Familia. The whole has an appropriately Daliesque feel.

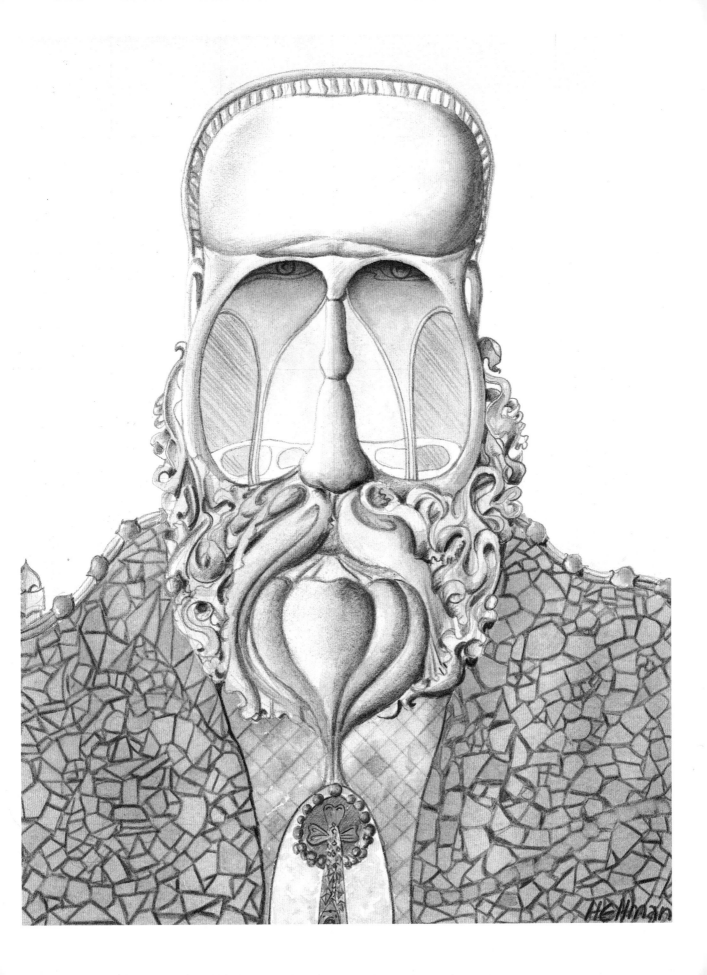

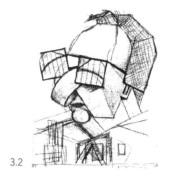

3.1

3.2

frank
gehry

**the guggenheim down in bilbao,
was inspired by a whale not a cao,
for something's fishy about gehry,
'form swallows function' is his theory.**

1

Frank O Gehry (1929), the Canadian architect based in Santa Monica, has gained international fame due to his Guggenheim Museum, Bilbao (1998). He is seen as the master exponent of Deconstructivism, a label he denies being free from the arcane theorising of the American avant-garde. Gehry's influences stem as much from pop artists like Rauschenberg and Oldenburg as architects such as Eames and Goff. All employed some aspect of collage, collating as-found materials not usually associated with 'proper' art and architecture. Gehry's extension to his own Santa Monica house (1970) initiated his assemblage style of different geometries and materials, galvanised metal, corrugated steel, ply, exposed studwork and especially chain-link. What followed was the very LA-influenced pop architecture to which Venturi had aspired. Since then, Gehry has gradually developed a more organic, homogeneous approach, reminiscent of Europeans like Scharoun, which evokes plant or animal forms, especially fish. Sculptural,

monumental, amorphous, a shimmering, titanium, beached whale, Bilbao is the culmination of this. It has already become a symbol for the city, tourist magnet and advert for US global cultural colonialism. Now every city aspires to having its own Bilbao. The complex shapes could only be resolved by computer technology but, being formed of cladding over steel frames, there is no structural logic to them. This is building as sculpture.

Gehry has a mischievous, cherubic appearance: uncontrollable white hair, prominent nose, thick-rimmed specs. He could be the Joker in *Batman* or the mad scientist in *Back to the Future*. The *Archi-tête*, which is pre-Bilbao, forms the head from the Vitra Chair Museum with Gehry's chain-link baffles for the hair. Part of the Edgemar Development in Santa Monica is the shirt and tie, and he clutches Oldenburg's giant binoculars from the Chiat Day Ad Agency. The mouth is, of course, a fish. Cod is in the details.

Stage 1
1. Preliminary caricatures from photographs

Stage 3
3.1 & 3.2 First freehand sketches

ostentation : (1) a pretentious and vulgar display esp. of wealth
and luxury. (2) the attempt or intention
to attract notice.
pariah : a social outcast.,
myopic (myopia : (1) short-sightedness
person.

3

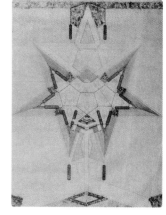

2

bruce
goff

bruce goff was a bit of a loner,
because he worked in oklahoma,
and thought architecture should be fun,
kind of 'annie get your mastic gun...'

7 12
1982
-1904
78

78yrs

Bruce Goff (1904–1982), self-taught, mid-Western friend and admirer of Frank Lloyd Wright, was considered an eccentric maverick by the US Modernist establishment. Operating from 'remote' Oklahoma, he had an office in Wright's Price Tower. Goff's buildings, mostly houses for clients with modest means, were highly individual and not related to any school or movement, although he was usually categorised under 'organic'. Yet he seems also to have pioneered a kind of junk, recycled technology transfer as well as self-build, his clients often participating in the construction. His designs, usually based on spirals, circles, hexagons and stars, incorporated all sorts of scavenged materials, including sewer pipes, Nissen huts, fly screens, oil rig parts, coal, bits of aeroplanes, carpet roofs and even goose feathers. Consequently, he was for a

time hailed as a hero of the 1960s recycling counter culture. Goff certainly personified the all-American celebration of individualism, consumerism, populism and 'dream home' ostentation, but from the perspective of the late 1990s, he is not so much a pariah as a prophet.

In old age, Goff had the air of some myopic insect with his thick glasses, huge ears and pointy chin. Perhaps there is a hint of William Burrows with whom he may be compared. The *Archi-tête* is composed of Goff's plan forms: hexagons for glasses, shingle roofs for cheeks, with Plunkett House windows for ears and the roof of the Harder House as hair. His shirt is patterned with house plans and the background is taken from the *Oklahoma* film record cover, 'Everything's up-to-date in Kansas City.'

Stage 1
1. Preliminary caricature from photographs

Stage 2
Study of building plans and architectural photographs
2. Plan for Bass house project, Tulsa

Stage 3
3. First freehand sketch

44

1

2

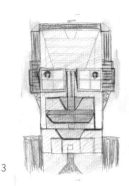

3

delved (delve; search energetically)
risible; laughable
ubiquitous: present everywhere or in several
places simultaneously

michael
graves

for michael graves' life is pretty hectic,
it's damned hard trying to be that eclectic,
exhuming dead styles is his pole totem,
not so much 'post-modern' as post-mortem.

Stage 1
1. Preliminary caricature from
photographs

Stage 2
Study of building plans and
architectural photographs
2. Humana headquarters,
Louisville

Stage 3
3. First freehand sketch

Michael Graves (1934) was, for a short time
the most fashionable of the American Post-
Modern Classicists. Operating from Princetown,
where he became professor, he first came to
prominence in 1972 as one of the New York
Five who resurrected Le Corbusier's 1920s
white purist houses as an applied style. Under
the influence of Leon Krier, Graves soon
abandoned the 'whites' for camp pastels and
delved further back into the past for imagery
adapting Schinkel, Boullée and Ledoux's
stripped Neo-Classicism, Olbrich, Hoffmann,
Art Deco Egyptian and so on. The resulting
mélange was seductive as pastel-coloured
drawings. However, his first large building,
the Portland Public Services HQ in Oregon
(1932), is a lumpen cube, ludicrously sham

and misconceived, with overblown *trompe l'œil*
effects painted on the facades (his mentor,
Philip Johnson, was on the competition jury).
His later work at Disneyland and elsewhere
is even more risible, described by the *New
York Times* as resembling 'some grotesque
architectural version of Alice after she
telescopes out into the giant world of
Wonderland.'

Graves looks like a cross between Dennis
Potter, Michael Howard and a shifty insect.
The *Archi-tête* portrays him as a version of
the Portland building with its painted swags
for eyes, the Graves ubiquitous inflated
keystone as forehead and tie, bits of stuck-on
High-Tech for ears, and the Humana building
for the jacket.

46

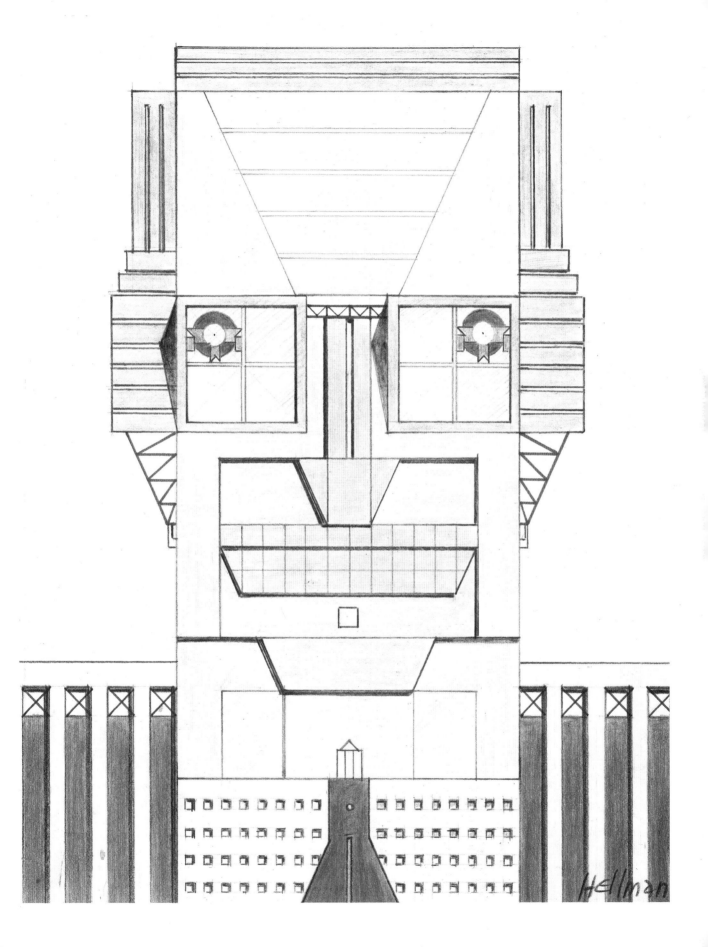

Hellman

3

2

nicholas
grimshaw

nick grimshaw's housing in camden town
might cause faint hearts to carp and frown,
me, i like living in a tin machine,
but then i'm a sainsbury's cooked sardine!

1

Nicholas Grimshaw (1939), the son of an aeronautical engineer, is, after Foster and Rogers, the most successful and inventive of the British High-Tech school in the tradition of Paxton and Brunel, with the obligatory obeisance to Prouvé, Eames and Fuller. Qualifying at the AA under Cedric Price and John Winter, Grimshaw formed an early partnership with Terry Farrell and in 1967 designed an Archigram-inspired 'plug-in' service tower (toilet block) for a London student hostel, a metal-clad block of private flats in Regent's Park (1968) and the Herman Miller factory outside Bath (1976). All High-Tech, but by 1980 Farrell had been seduced by Post-Modernism and the couple split to form their own practices and go on to greater things. Grimshaw designed the *Financial Times* Headquarters (now abandoned) and buildings for Sainsbury's, a Homebase in Brentford and a store in Camden Town plus some canal-side housing.

He shot to prominence with the Piano-inspired British Pavilion at the Seville Expo of 1992 and the glass-enveloped Waterloo Euroterminal, a snaking, zoomorphic celebration of flexible differential movement technology, since when the practice has taken off internationally. Grimshaw's serviced sheds are characterised by fine attention to detail and careful assemblage of components. Articulated like vertebrae, his buildings have latterly become less formal in the fashionable fusion of Functionalism and Expressionism mode. What is often lacking is the human content. There is a certain coldness and obsession with technique, a hall-mark of High-Tech perhaps, exemplified by the Camden Town housing.

Grimshaw's appearance is reminiscent of the engineer/boffin (or perhaps those comic noses with glasses and moustaches attached you get in joke shops): round, steel-rimmed glasses, walrus moustache and lock of hair falling perpetually across the forehead. The *Archi-tête* has a cladding panel from the Camden Town housing and a Waterloo truss as hair, windows from the FT building as glasses, a stanchion from Homebase as nose and moustache, the towers from the Runnymeade warehouse, Windsor as ears and cladding from Sainsbury's in Camden Town as jacket.

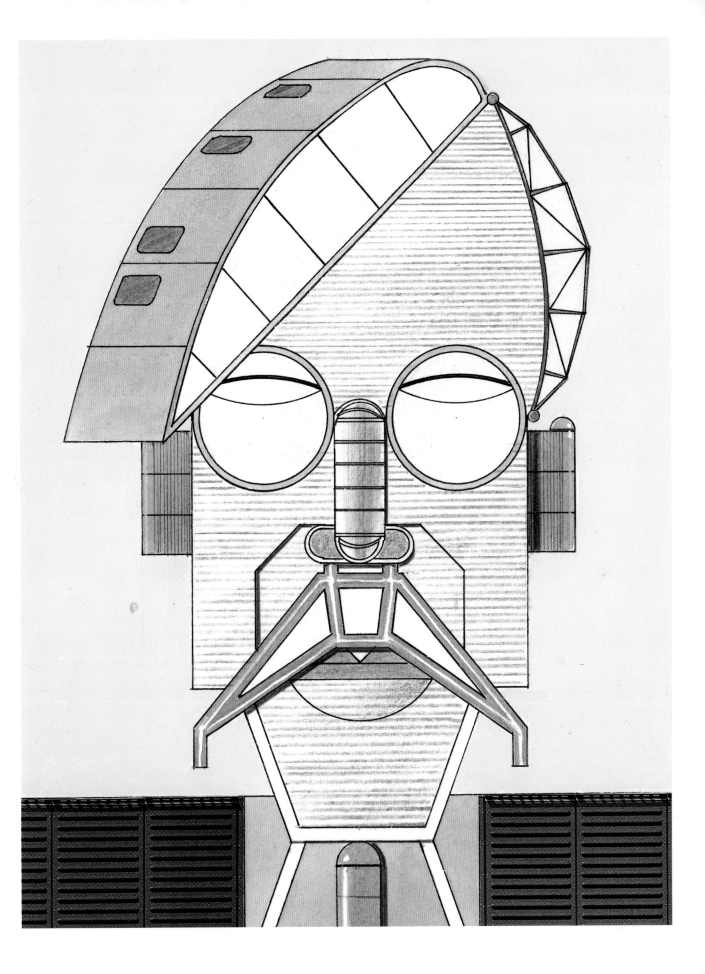

2

3

walter
gropius

1

at the bauhaus, gropius was the hub,
later on he designed our playboy club,
quite a progression from cones, spheres and cubes,
to bunny girls with big ears, tails and boobs!

Walter Gropius (1883–1969) was one of the great German pioneers of the Modern Movement and director of the famous Bauhaus design school, first in Weimar, then in Dessau from 1925 where he designed a complex of buildings to house the establishment. Gropius had already established the Machine Age style with Meyer in the Fagus Factory (1911), with its flat roof, framed structure, standard mass-produced parts and prototype glass curtain wall which wrapped around the building's corners. These ingredients were augmented and refined in the Bauhaus buildings, which influenced modern architecture for decades afterwards. With the rise to power of the Nazis, Gropius came to England, but the ethos was not supportive of radical Modernism and he went on to the USA where he had been offered a professorship at Harvard. Here he formed the Architects Collaborative in accordance with his ideal of teamworking. As with other pioneers who went to America, Gropius' socialist principles were soon shed and he even designed the London Playboy Club.

Tom Wolfe describes him as 'thirty-six-years old, slender, simply but meticulously groomed, with his thick black hair combed straight back, irresistibly handsome to women, correct in a classic German manner, a lieutenant of cavalry during the [first] war... Strictly speaking he was not an aristocrat, since his father, while well-to-do, was not of the nobility, but people couldn't help thinking of him as one. The painter Paul Klee... called Gropius "The Silver Prince".' The *Archi-tête* shows him around this age, based on an axonometric drawing of the Bauhaus with a Fagus Factory doorway ear. There is some resemblance to Dr Frankenstein's monster in the caricature and this seems appropriate to Gropius' rather cold Prussian mien. There was something of the night about him.

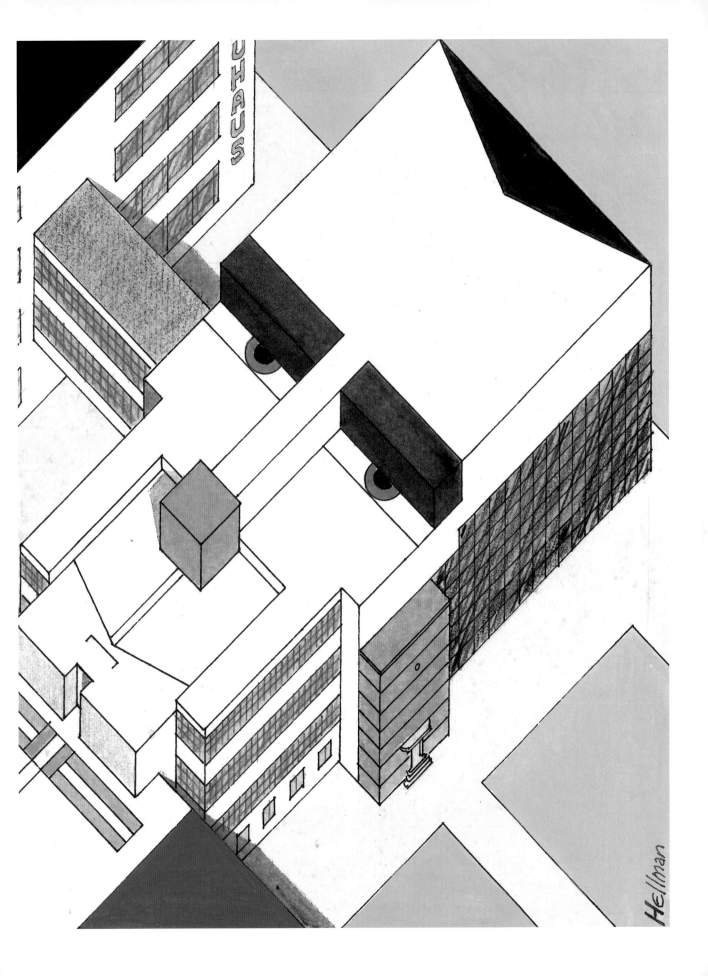

Hellman

3

2

1

hector
guimard

**that monsieur hector guimard,
was on the surface a dreamard,
but became very hetero,
when he went down the metero.**

Stage 1
1. Preliminary caricature from photographs

Stage 2
Study of building plans and architectural photographs
2. Entrance to the Metro, Paris

Stage 3
3. First freehand sketch

Hector Guimard (1867–1942) was the main French Art Nouveau architect influenced both by Horta, the Belgian originator, and the structural possibilities of cast iron developed by Viollet-le-Duc. His major works in Paris include the eclectic Castel Béranger apartment block (1898), the Humbert-de-Romans building (1902) with its impressive cast-iron interior, and especially his designs for the entrances to Metro stations. Some of these still exist, the sinuous, plant-derived cast-iron forms of the new art serving the new transport technology. Guimard transformed the structural elements of buildings as well as railings, balustrades and furniture into highly charged images of great individual richness and refinement.

From the sparse photographic evidence, the young Guimard's appearance typified the flamboyant, *fin de siècle*, cultured artist. With his sensuously curled moustache, beard and hair he might have stepped out of a painting by Toulouse-Lautrec or Degas. This *Archi-tête* shows Guimard as a variation on his famous wrought-iron doors to the Castel Béranger. Mind the doors!

52

Hellman

zaha
hadid

an architect name of zaha
drives a deconstructed green car,
when she's asked how it feels,
on triangular wheels,
replies, 'dahlink, i've saved thousands on petrol so far.'

Stage 1
1. Preliminary caricature from photographs

Stage 2
Study of building plans and architectural photographs
2. Vitra Fire Station in Weil am Rhein, Germany

Stage 3
3. First freehand sketch

Zaha Hadid (1950), an Iraqi based in London, is one of the leading exponents of the current Deconstructivist style of architecture. She studied in Beirut and at the AA in London where she was encouraged by Rem Koolhaas. She achieved international fame by winning the (unbuilt) Hong Kong Peak competition (1983) for a leisure centre, thanks to Isozaki who was on the jury, with a dynamic design reviving Russian Constructivism and Suprematist paintings. Hadid then became an international star by virtue of her drawings which disdain the conventions of architectural communication and are splintered, layered, fragmented and streamlined, as well as being incomprehensible as blueprints for building construction. She aims at an unattainable zero gravity, a weightless architecture in motion. Unfortunately, when her first buildings appeared, such as the Vitra Fire Station (1994), the gulf between drawn intent and constructed reality was greater than usual.

The Station uses old solid materials like concrete in the fashionable but wilfully vertiginous mode where nothing is vertical or horizontal. Hadid then won the competition for the Cardiff Opera House but was shamefully blocked by national politics, local misogyny and racism. Thus, she acquired all the prerequisites of the misunderstood, martyred genius as well as a lot of colour supplement publicity. She is now building in Japan, Berlin, Cincinnati and Rome.

Hadid has the pyramidic appearance of a mountainous Miyake-clad Madonna or Mona Lisa, with long auburn hair, round lidded eyes, long nose, sensuous mouth and sexy/husky voice. She has been described as a cross between Cruella de Vil and Zsa Zsa Gabor but Mitterand's view of Mrs Thatcher as having the eyes of Caligula and the mouth of Marilyn Monroe might be more apt. The Archi-tête vainly tries to reconcile Hadid's spikey drawings and fleshy mien with hair based on the Peak hillside.

2

3.1

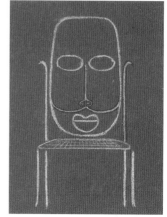

3.2

josef
hoffmann

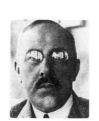

four architects' names end in 'man',
i can name you each of the clan,
there's brygg, eisen and port,
at the back of one's thought,
but hoff, he was garde of the van.

1

Stage 1
1. Preliminary caricature from photographs

Stage 2
Study of building plans and architectural photographs
2. Sitzmaschine

Stage 3
3.1 & 3.2 First freehand sketches

Josef Hoffmann (1870–1956) was, with Adolf Loos, one of the foremost Austrian architects who made the transition from the *Jugendstil* to early Modernism. A disciple of Otto Wagner, Hoffmann was one of the founding architect members (with Olbrich) of the breakaway Vienna Secession and in 1903 formed the Wiener Werkstatte with Koloman Moser. Influenced by the English Arts and Crafts, its remit was to design, produce and market high-quality domestic objects, particularly chairs, for the bourgeoisie. His major building was the Palais Stoclet (1905) built for a wealthy Brussels family to serve as luxury mansion, museum and beacon of fashionable taste. Its

black and white orthogonal treatment was a precursor of Miesian Modernism, evoking an exclusive way of life in its imagery and mood, a sort of 'aristocratic bohemianism' soon to be swept away by the First World War. Hoffmann always employed decorative devices and was thus later condemned by the hard liner Loos.

Hoffmann's appearance is somewhat military early on: typical *fin-de-siècle* handlebar moustache, rimless spectacles and cropped hair. Later, he looks rather like a professor of psychology, a follower of Freud perhaps? The *Archi-tête* has him as a version of one of his bentwood chair designs with decorative designs for the body. A trifle sinister!

56

Hellman

1

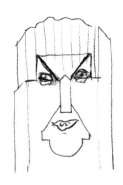

3

2

hans
hollein

herr hans hollein
is doing fine,
and doesn't shirk
gesamtkunstwerk.

Stage 1
1. Preliminary caricature from photographs

Stage 2
Study of building plans and architectural photographs
2. Mönchengladbach Museum, Germany

Stage 3
3. First freehand sketch

Hans Hollein (1934) is the foremost Austrian Post-Modernist, very much in the Viennese Baroque and *Jugendstil* tradition of fusing fine art, design and architecture. Hollein studied in Vienna and the USA, and first gained attention with his aircraft carrier city, a loony 1960s megastructure. In Vienna, he built up his practice designing shop fronts, interiors and exhibitions. He turned to Post-Modernism, notably at the 1980 Venice Biennale, with his heavy-handedly ironic 'crassical' portico, 'Neon Unites Columns'. The Austrian Travel Bureau (1978) is also crammed full of symbolism and ironic metaphor with references to Nash and Lutyens, among others, and joke Rolls Royce grilles to the cashiers, all verging on whimsy but beautifully detailed. Hollein has since avoided much of the crassness of Post-Modernism by the use of high-quality materials — marble, stone, brass and zinc — employed in new ways and

peppered with historic references. He has now inevitably moved into museum design. His new museum in Mönchengladbach is conceived as an artificial landscape built into a hillside and that in Frankfurt as a slice of *kasekuchen* on a wedged-shaped site. Internally, both exhibit a succession of stunning spaces.

Hollein is an artist but is certainly no oil painting, with piggy eyes, fleshy face, piano keys for teeth and a balding pate. It is hard not to imagine him in Second World War uniform. The *Archi-tête* appropriately is built up of references to several buildings: Mönchengladbach for the head, the Schullin jewellery shop for the mouth, the Haas shopping centre for the body, the Schullin ll front door as tie, and one of the travel bureau palm tree columns as buttonhole. Then there's that embarrassing aircraft carrier on his shoulder. A monster talent!

Hellman

2

1

3

arata
isozaki

a isozaki
mixes up pomo d'oro,
with sukiaki.

Arata Isozaki (1931) is the most prolific of the Japanese Post-Modern 'new wave'. He first worked for Kenzo Tange designing Corb-inspired Brutalism but added overtones of traditional Japanese framed buildings. In 1960, he set up on his own and was bracketed with the Metabolist movement which, like Archigram, proposed advanced technology and social mobility in Utopian projects related to Japanese industrial expansion and the consequent influence of the West. Maintaining that Japanese architecture had always borrowed from the outside, Isozaki began to incorporate elements from the European Renaissance and Neo-Classicism. These were often combined with Modernist gridded geometric forms in an eclectic, collaged, self-consciously arty style, employing crude or obscure metaphor, such as in the

Fujima Country Club (1974) whose plan form is a question mark and entrance a stripped Palladio reference. In the 1980s, he adopted the full American Post-Modern style in his Tsukuba Civic Centre (1982), a bewildering *mélange* of historic quotations, and later in his Florida building for Disney which is pure Mousitecture. Isozaki has since changed tack again in favour of High-Tech grids where historic forms play a subsidiary role. 'Architecture as a pleasure machine.'

Isozaki's appearance has progressed from 1960s freaked-out Three Stooges look to quizzical elder statesman. The *Archi-tête* pitches him around the middle, with Disney-style hair; face, eyes, eyebrows and mouth taken from Tsukuba; jacket and tie from Disney again; and historic elements, a pyramid and a Boulléesque rising sun, as shoulder pads.

Hellman

3

2

philip
johnson

1

philip johnson predicts, and he should know, that the prima donna era must go, and a sentiment he surely condones is: those in glass houses should not throw stones.

Philip Johnson (1906), the New York-based nonagenarian, is a type of architectural chameleon. The son of a wealthy lawyer, when he was twenty-eight, he donated money to the Museum of Modern Art (instituted by rich patrons to promote the European avant-garde) to set up an architecture unit, which he headed, and for which he later designed new galleries. In 1932, he mounted an influential exhibition with Henry-Russell Hitchcock entitled 'The International Style' which proclaimed European Functionalism as a universal *aesthetic*, stripped of any social or political context. In 1949, Johnson designed his famous glass house in the Miesian mode and then preceded to indulge in whatever style was fashionable; Miesian for the Seagram building, neo-fascist for the Lincoln Center, Louis Kahn for the Yale Laboratories and so on. When

Post-Modernism came along in the 1980s, Johnson leapt to the forefront with his AT&T skyscraper which was essentially a standard modern slab with out-of-scale mock Classical elements stuck on, the very thing he had condemned in 1932! A succession of similar corporate buildings followed, some mock Classical, some mock Gothic and Johnson became a god-father figure/patron to the 'young' PoMos. Now in his nineties, he is designing in the current fashion for Deconstruction.

Johnson's appearance in old age resembles a crafty old reptile: suave, sophisticated,urbane, rich. Cynical eyes penetrate his familiar, thick, round, black-framed, Corb-style glasses. The *Archi-tête* shows him as a group of his standard skyscrapers with various applied Post-Modern tops.

Stage 1
1. Preliminary caricature from photographs

Stage 2
Study of building plans and architectural photographs
2. Model of the AT&T building, New York

Stage 3
3. First freehand sketch

Hellman

1

3

2

louis
кahn

they say that louis кahn
just didn't give a darn,
he'd pull most awful faces,
in served and servant spaces.

Stage 1
1. Preliminary caricature from
photographs

Stage 2
Study of building plans and
architectural photographs
2. Buildings designed for the capital of
East Pakistan

Stage 3
3. First freehand sketch

Louis Kahn (1901–1974), born in Estonia, was
the leading architect in the USA to make the
transition from International Style Functionalism
to a revival of formalism and monumentality,
known initially as New Brutalism (ugh). His Yale
University Art Gallery (1953) concealed its
framed structure, previously always expressed
according to Miesian principles, behind panels
of brickwork with the floor levels expressed
on the outside as string courses. Heresay!
The gallery was open plan with the stairs,
lifts and toilets contained in a separate zone.
This developed into the notion of served
and servant spaces in the Richards Medical
Research Building, Philadelphia (1957–60)
where the stairs, ducts and services are
housed in monumental San Gimignano-like
brick towers separated from the laboratories.
This idea did not really work but has since
influenced architects like Richard Rogers –

even today. Kahn's later designs, like the
Government Centre at Dacca (1973–76),
attempted to evolve an elemental, geometric,
hierarchical formal language based on
archetypal historic precedent. It represented
a break with dogmatic Functionalism and
paved the way for Post-Modernists like Botta,
Rossi and Stirling.

Tom Wolfe described Kahn as, 'A grey little
man … He was short. He had wispy reddish-
white hair that stuck out this way and that.
His face was badly scarred as the result of
a childhood accident. He wore wrinkled shirts
and black suits… His tie was always loose.
He was nearsighted… you would see Kahn
holding some student's yard-long blueprint
three inches from his face and moving his head
over it like a scanner.' This *Archi-tête* presents
four myopic Louis Kahns arranged like one
of his axial Beaux-Arts plans *à la* Dacca.

64

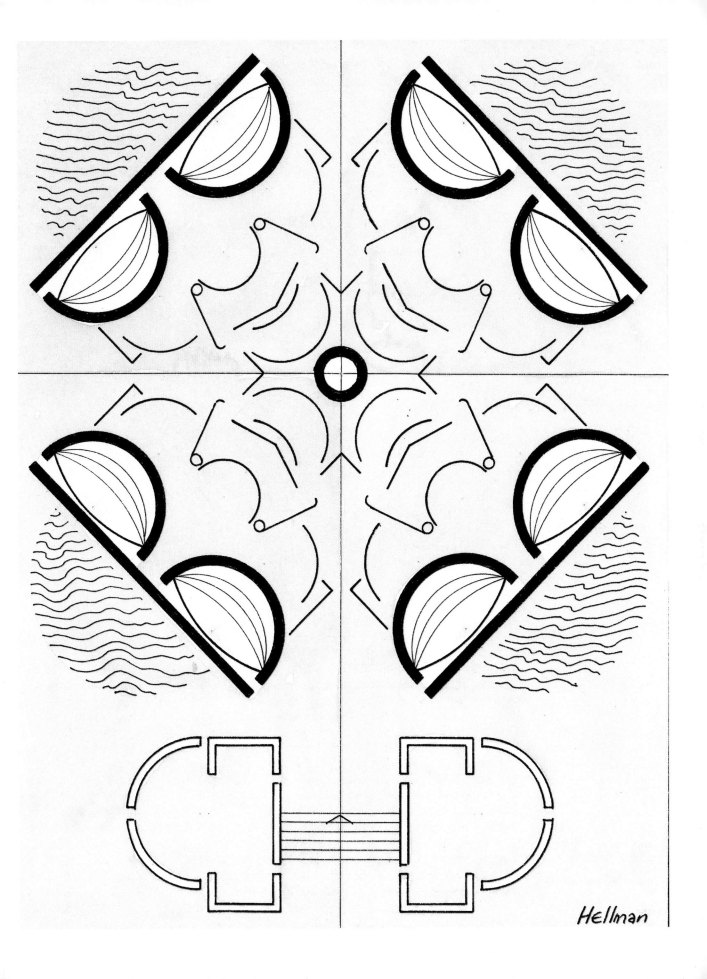

Hellman

1

3

2

rem koolhaas

i can't understand all the palaver,
about rem koolhaas' villa dall'ava,
the sides are quite dotty,
on potty pilotis,
quite the opposite of calatrava.

Stage 1
1. Preliminary caricature from photographs

Stage 2
Study of building plans and architectural photographs
2. Villa Dall'Ava in Paris

Stage 3
3. First freehand sketch

Rem Koolhaas (1944) is London-based and educated Dutch architect and book maker. His work is hard to classify, being a kind of Post-Modern, ad-hoc, deconstructed Brutalism using cheap modern materials, *à la* early Gehry, such as polyester, fibreglass, corrugated steel or aluminium, raw concrete and Astroturf, in a consciously 'unpretentious' and 'unsentimental' manner. In 1975, he helped found the portentous sounding Office of Metropolitan Architecture (OMA) and first came to prominence with his book *Delirious New York*, a sort of collage comic paean to Manhattan. Since then, his work has graduated from small, medium and large to extra large, and spawned Arquitectonica and Zaha Hadid. The apolitical Koolhaas cites his influences as the Neo-Suprematism of Leonidov and neo-plasticism, but the pop/constructivist graphics often do not translate very adequately into buildings.

These tend to be simultaneously cold and overdone, much play with gratuitous ramps, angles and awkwardly clashing materials. No doubt Koolhaas would insist this was his aim. He described his master plan for EuraLille and one of its core buildings, the Congrexpo (ugh!), as 'the dynamics of hell'. It is certainly hell trying to find your way round it!

Koolhaas is tall, bony, intense, dog-faced, tight lipped, virtually bald with projecting ears, bulgy eyes and a crooked nose. The *Archi-tête* is based around the Villa Dall'Ava, Paris, which he designed for a rich disabled aesthete. The projecting blue and red corrugated-clad wings on those potty pilotis (which have since become a cliché for Deconstructivists) serve as ears, the blue one-lane, roof-top pool as vestigial hair and the strip windows as eyebrows and eyes. The nose is vaguely EuraLille and the shoulders from the Congrexpo metal and glass cladding.

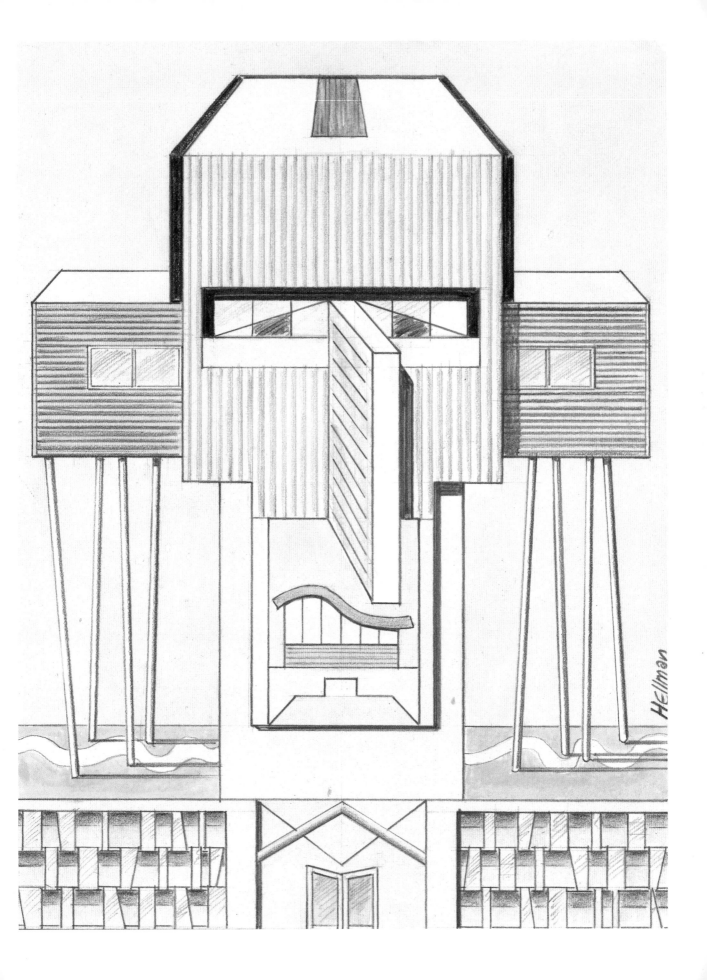

Hellman

le
corbusier

le corbusier was mr clean,
a house to him was just a machine,
and when the owners started to grouse,
he redesigned them to fit the house.

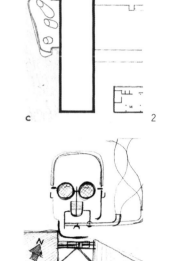

2

LE CORBUSIER   Hellmu   3.2

1

3.1

Stage 1
1. Preliminary caricature from
photographs

Stage 2
Study of building plans and
architectural photographs
2. Plan of la Tourette Eveux-sur-
l'Arbresle

Stage 3
3.1 & 3.2 First freehand sketches

Le Corbusier (1887–1965), a Swiss French working in Paris, was the most inventive and influential of the pioneers of the Modern Movement from the 1920s to the 1960s. His ideas were reinforced by polemic and painting, like Picasso to whom he may be compared. Le Corbusier drew on diverse influences from Classicism, the vernacular, North African culture, the Mediterranean, mass-produced machine technology, the Werkbund, Perret's reinforced concrete structures and nineteenth-century philosophy, often changing direction as a result. Most modern architectural ideas can be traced back to Le Corbusier's projects, including the machine aesthetic, Functionalism, neo-vernacular, eco/organic, Post- Modernism and Deconstructivism. At the same time, his attempts at rationalisation tended to disintegrate or compartmentalise much like separating out the parts of a Swiss watch. This can be seen in his arbitrary five points for a new architecture (pilotis, roof gardens, free plan, free facades and strip windows) and in his ideal city plans with their obsession for the ordered zoning of functions, both of which have had a huge and often detrimental influence. Despite crude Functionalist slogans like, 'A house is a machine for living in' (which in reality meant buildings aping the form of ships or planes), the 1920s iconic 'white' houses for affluent aesthetes in Parisian suburbs (which employed mainly traditional

building methods to mimic smooth machine age forms) are spatial poems of intense creativity and were copied sheep-like by architects the world over. The Pavillon Suisse hostel (1932), incorporating raw concrete pilotis and rubble walling, however, signalled a change in direction.

Born Charles-Edouard Jeanneret, the name Le Corbusier was adapted from his grandmother's *nom de jeune fille* as a not very good pun on the French word for a raven, *le corbeau*. Especially in his younger days, 'Corb' as he is known to architects, had a distinctly bird-like appearance: round-rimmed, black, owlish glasses, slicked back hair and beaky nose. His characteristic sallow complexion, intense gaze (so useful for Futurist predictions), bow tie (slightly arty), pipe (practicality) and dark suits (business-like) marked him out as the archetypal machine age 'engineeritect' and his austere, stiff, humourless Calvinist mien (he disliked children) chimed well with the Puritanical doctrines of the Functionalists.

This *Archi-tête*, the first to be created, presents Corb as one of his typical pre-war house plans with characteristic toilet forms for spectacles and eyes, stairs for nose, La Tourette chapel as ear and a ramp for pipe. The bow tie is one of the Pavillon Suisse pilotis and the pocket a bed for Modular Man, the pin-headed, Frankenstein-like figure who was Corb's idealised building user.

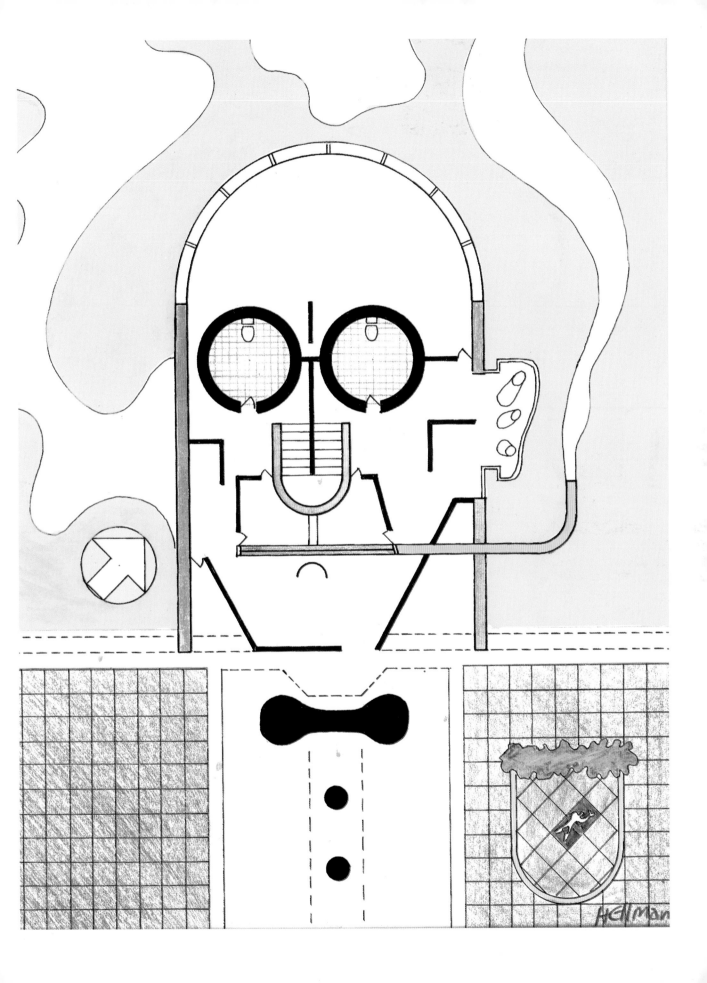

Hellman

1

3

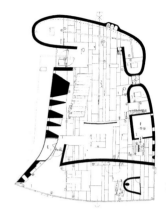

2

le corbusier (late)

**an architect went to heaven and rejoiced,
'isn't that corb i see over there?', he voiced,
'no, you're mistaken', he heard st peter say,
'that's god, he just thinks he's le corbusier!'**

After the war, during which he collaborated with the Vichy regime (his 'apolitical technocrat' position meant he sought work from power bases whether extreme left or right), Le Corbusier's style altered course radically. Whether as a result of the rapid deterioration of the 'machine-age' houses, with their cracked white render, rusting frames and lack of drips and cornices (now mostly museums due to the cost of maintenance), or because of a philosophical shift to the vernacular, his buildings now employed raw concrete (*béton brut*) straight from the shutter in monumental forms which would 'weather' like traditional materials. As ever, the architect sheep converted in droves to copy the new style which became known as Brutalism. In 1947, Corb was commissioned by the Socialist mayor of Marseilles to build a *Unité*, a monumental block of workers' apartments on massive pilotis, which incorporated all the support facilities – shops, restaurants, playgrounds, sports areas – like a small town. The concept was based on the nineteenth-century philosopher Fourier's vision of the *Phalanstère,* or idealised socialist commune,

an isolating and patronising solution handed down from on high to be cheapened and repeated in thousands of housing estates around the world. The private Maisons Jaoul (1956) jammed in between lumpen blocks in Neuilly and using the same technology are superb by contrast. However, when it came to religious buildings, like the Chapel at Ronchamp (1954) or La Tourette monastery (1960), the old atheist delivered masterpieces, particularly the former which is the most beautiful of all modern churches. Organic and Greek vernacular inspired, it is structurally entirely 'dishonest' – but then, architects rarely practice what they preach.

As his buildings became rough in texture, so Corb's features became craggy and lined with advancing age, resembling now a buzzard rather than a raven (*Le Busier?*). Symbolically, Corb drowned while swimming in the Mediterranean, the source of many of his post-war architectural ideas. Modular Man is dead, long live Non-Standard Person! The second *Archi-tête* is a deconstructed collage or *découpage* of the Ronchamp chapel plan.

Stage 1
1. Preliminary caricature from photographs

Stage 2
Study of building plans and architectural photographs
2. Plan of Ronchamp Chapel, Notre Dame-du-Haut

Stage 3
3. First freehand sketch

Hellman

2

3

daniel
libeskind

1

**daniel libeskind has designed a spiral
at the v&a which looks quite viral,
prince albert would no doubt have enthused,
but queen victoria is not amused.**

Stage 1
1. Preliminary caricature from photographs

Stage 2
Study of building plans and architectural photographs
2. Jewish Museum in Berlin

Stage 3
3. First freehand sketch

Daniel Libeskind (1946), the Polish/American Deconstructivist architect working in Berlin, specialises in winning competitions for major museum extensions. A Mozart-style musical child prodigy, he won a scholarship to study in New York where he abandoned Mahler for mathematics and then architecture. After the obligatory 'radical avant-garde' visiting professorships and stunningly oblique drawings, Libeskind won the competitions to design an extension to the Berlin Jewish Museum in 1989 and a wing devoted to the Jewish painter Felix Nussbaum at the Osnabruck Museum. In both cases, the buildings-as-sculpture-with-a-message attempt to rationalise their deconstructed forms by simplistic narrative references based on contextual and topographical connections. The resulting galleries tend to be a nightmare for curators, since the architecture dominates the contents, as witnessed by the huge popularity of the Berlin museum before any exhibits were placed. In 1998, Libeskind won the competition to design a small but expensive extension to London's V&A Museum with a vertiginous box-framed spiral. The structure of this was resolved by the engineer Cecil Balmond, citing rather dubious fractal principles, with fractal-patterned tiling as external decoration. As with Bilbao, this is museum as 'stunning' advert and tourist magnet, over-designed, out of context and employing a kind of deconstructed facadism draped around a fairly ordinary plan. Naturally, Libeskind is now an international star building more museums in Manchester and elsewhere.

Libeskind is a hyperactive, garrulous, bumptious, self-styled 'genius', rather like the Mozart character in *Amadeus* or Jerry Lewis on speed, all teeth, hair and glasses. The *Archi-tête* conceives him as a version of the V&A spiral with frac-tiling on the hair and the plan of the Berlin Museum serving as teeth. Wunderkind!

1

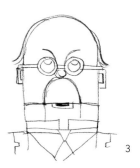
3

2

sir edwin
lutyens

detailing by lutyens,
right down to escutcheons,
turns critics to jelly,
from drogo to delhi.

Sir Edwin Landseer Lutyens (1869–1944)
could be described as the architectural
equivalent of Elgar; both combined an English
romanticism with Edwardian imperial pomp. He
began his career with a series of opulent
country houses designed under the influence of
the late Arts and Crafts movement, especially
figures such as Shaw and Webb. In 1896,
Lutyens met the great landscape gardener
Gertrude Jekyll and began a long professional
relationship whereby house and garden design
were integrated. Unlike Voysey or Mackintosh,
Lutyens adopted the post-war fashion for Neo-
Classicism, often combining it with Arts and
Crafts elements. Later, he dabbled in neo-
Georgian or Queen Anne (jokingly referring to it
as his 'Wrennaissance') for banks, commercial
buildings and luxury homes for the wealthy,
such as Castle Drogo. He was adopted as
official establishment architect designing war

memorials like the London Cenotaph,
embassies and especially the master plan for
new Delhi and the Viceroy's House there in
mock Hindu temple neo-colonial style. Lutyens
was not an innovator but a superb manipulator
of existing styles, whether Arts and Crafts or
Neo-Classical, and this is possibly why he was
neglected after the Second World War until he
was 'discovered' and reinstated by the 1970s
Post-Modernist movement.

In appearance, Lutyens was bald, owlish
behind his round spectacles, and sported the
obligatory Edwardian moustache. He had a fine
sense of humour and his letters are peppered
with witty cartoons and caricatures. This
Archi-tête shows him as one of his early
symmetrical houses with a touch of half
timbering at the ears, bullseye windows for
glasses and the dome of the Viceroy's House
for a cranium.

74

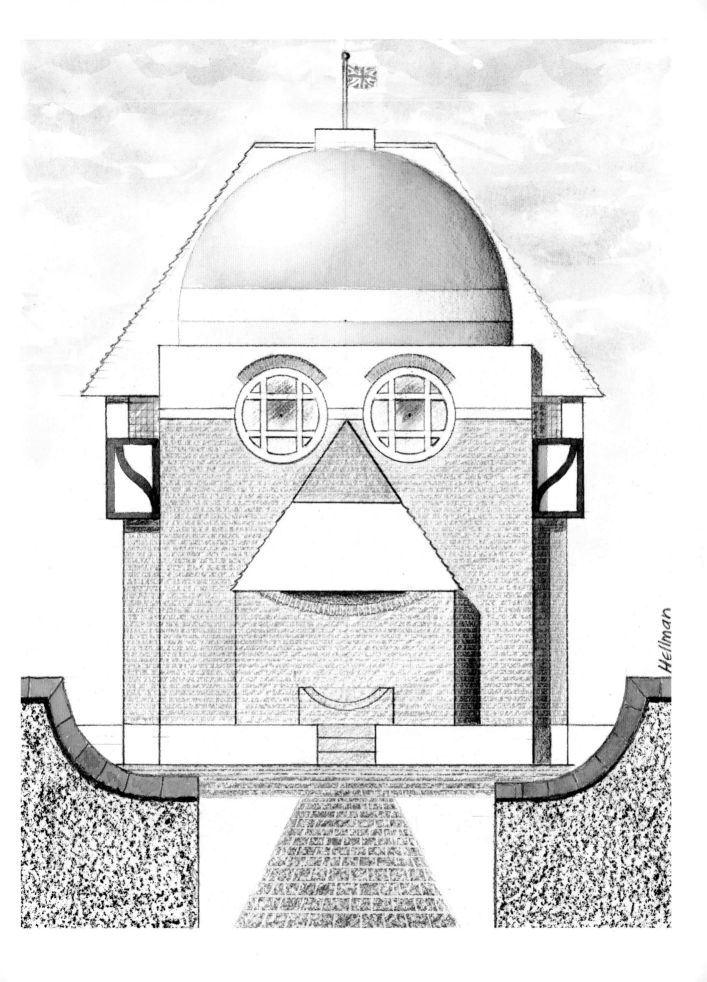

Hellman

3

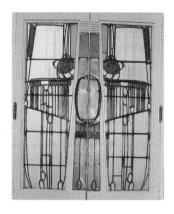

2

charles rennie

mackintosh

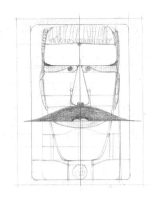

young charles rennie mackintosh was smart,
he designed the glasgow school of art,
pure genius, so the scots made sure
he never built anything anymore.

Stage 1
1. Preliminary caricature from photographs

Stage 2
Study of building plans and architectural photographs
2. Door to Willow Tea Rooms, Glasgow

Stage 3
3. First freehand sketch

Charles Rennie Mackintosh (1868–1928) was the leading architect in Glasgow of the British Art Nouveau movement, combining Arts and Crafts, the Scottish Baronial tradition and the sensual curves of the new art. His masterpiece is the Glasgow School of Art (1898–1907), which exemplifies this approach and is to this day functional and robust enough to withstand the onslaught of art students while, at the same time, incorporating refined detailing. Mackintosh designed two stunning houses and the interiors of several tea rooms, but he never did another major public building. He was fêted in Vienna and Germany, but ignored in his home country where the architectural establishment never honoured him. After the First World War, Mackintosh and his wife and partner Margaret McDonald, who is rarely given sufficient credit, left for England and France but built almost nothing more.

Since the 1980s, Mackintosh has been 'discovered' by his home town and Glasgow is rife with pseudo 'Tackintosh' design. How he would have loathed it.

Mackintosh's appearance, in his younger incarnation, typified the *fin de siècle*, romantic, arty, anti-establishment code of the time, long curly hair, big moustache, billowing cravats to florid Art Nouveau designs, and thick tweed suits. This *Archi-tête* is based on Mackintosh's famous stained-glass doors to the Willow Tea Rooms in Sauchiehall Street. Miss Cranston's tea rooms were intended to attract the working classes away from the pubs and demon drink (some hope in Glasgow). It is ironic that she chose an architect who was a whisky addict. In fact, the doors and mirror frieze in the rooms are positively psychedelic (or intoxicating?) when seen at a rapid glance. Spooky!

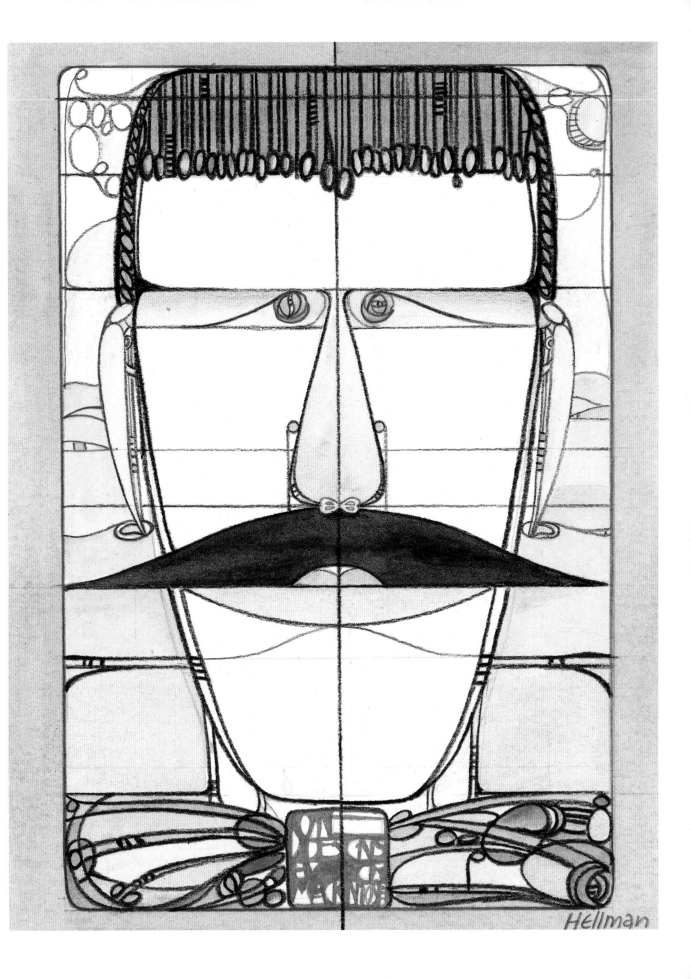

Hellman

1

2

imre
makovecz

quick, go and fetch that makovecz, his church just ate my favourite pet.

3

Imre Makovecz (1935), the Hungarian son of a carpenter, has brought new vigour to the traditions of National Romanticism and organic architecture in a kind of Post-Modern mode equivalent to the music of Pärt or Górecki. The cliché of 'maverick' or 'crank' is often applied to him, due to his opposition to mainstream Modernism. This was not merely aesthetic but political and dangerous, since it represents opposition to the state style imposed by the puppet communist regime until 1989. Makovecz was consequently ostracised by the party from the 1960s and worked on small rural projects influenced by Rudolf Steiner's notions of the *genius loci*, the Hungarian vernacular, nature and religion as symbols of freedom. The strange, bulbous, zoomorphic and anthropomorphic forms of his buildings, especially the churches, using a vocabulary derived from upturned boats, skulls, beehives, Magyar helmets and even wings are unclassifyable but aspects of Wright, Aalto, Gaudí, Goff, Dutch

Expressionism and Eisenstein's cinema are present. His innovative use of various kinds of structural timber, random weather boarding and shingles as well as carving, stained glass and natural light give the buildings a brooding surreal menace on the edge of folksy kitsch. Now honoured in his own country, Makovecz came to international notice through his 1992 Seville Expo pavilion with its cluster of spires and symbolic finials.

Makovecz has a typical dour, morose, East European mien yet is chubby and avuncular with the obligatory Walensa moustache, bald pate and narrow Slav eyes. The *Archi-tête* shows him as a version of one of his churches, with the double S-shape (a typical ying/yang type of symbolic pattern in Hungarian folk art) from the Siofok Lutheran church forming the eyebrows, nose and cheeks, while the hair is a version of the wings framing the entrance to the same building. Random boarding, as used on the Páks Catholic church for cladding, forms the moustache.

Stage 1
1. Preliminary caricature from photographs

Stage 2
Study of building plans and architectural photographs
2. Siofok Church, Hungary

Stage 3
3. First freehand sketch

78

Hellman

2

3

richard
meier

richard meier,
in white attire,
a francophile,
of purist guile,
he had his way,
with jeanneret.

1

Richard Meier (1934), the White Knight of Post-Modernism, worked for SOM and Marcel Breuer before opening his own office in New York in 1963. His work first consisted of houses for the wealthy and he came to prominence as one of the New York Five exhibited at MOMA in 1969. The five 'whites', as opposed to Venturi and the 'greys', revived the heroic white period of Rietveld, Gropius, Terragni and especially Le Corbusier, but as applied aesthetics stripped of any social commitment. Meier's houses, all white on green-field sites, play games with vertical and horizontal layering derived from Corb's purist period. This variation on a theme was later inflated and applied to museum commissions in Atlanta, Frankfurt, LA, Paris and Barcelona. These whitened sepulchres are invariably compositions of enamelled white panels, frames and glass making much play with ramps and circulation in the American museum manner, often at the expense of function. The marketing advantage is that a Meier building is instantly brand identifiable. However, the Paris Opéra de la Bastille competition winner appeared to be a Meier entry but was found to be someone else's pastiche of a Meier pastiche of Le Corbusier with disastrous consequences.

Meier in middle age looks like a well-fed German chancellor, intense gaze behind thin-rimmed specs, predatory mouth, double chin, longish white hair. This *Archi-tête* presents him as one of his axonometric museum renderings, whiter than white of course.

80

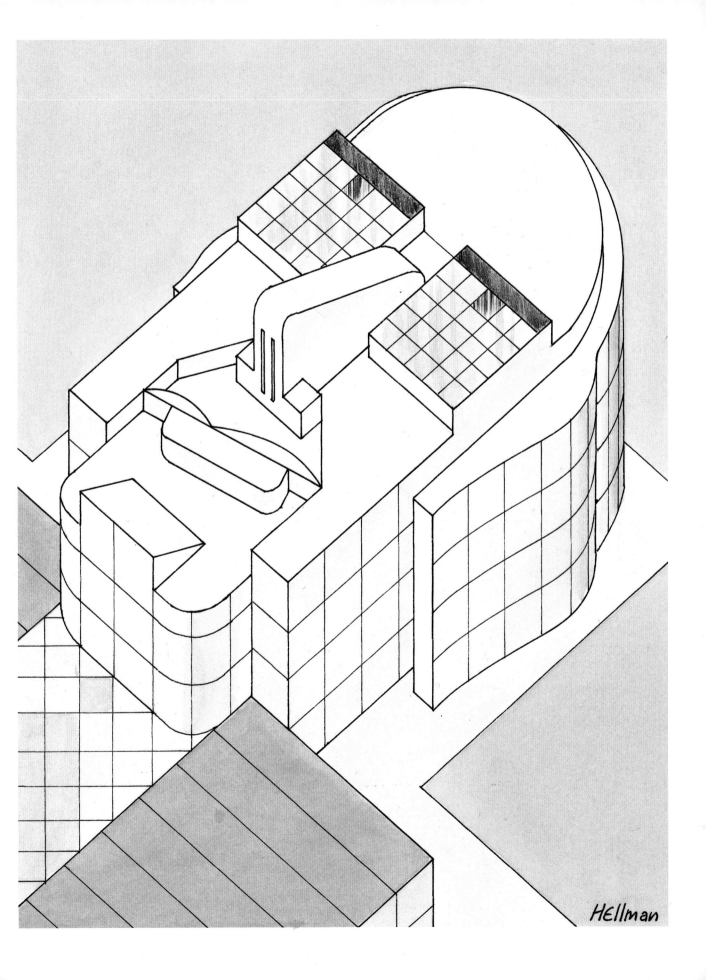

HEllman

2

1

3

erich
mendelsohn

Stage 1
1. Preliminary caricature from photographs

Stage 2
Study of building plans and architectural photographs
2. Study for an optical factory

Stage 3
3. First freehand sketch

Erich Mendelsohn (1887–1953) was one of the principal architects of the German Expressionist movement and was early on associated with the Blaue Reiter group which included Klee, Kandinsky and Marc. He produced many projects for dynamic Expressionist buildings in a bold black-and-white style and, after serving in the First World War, opened an office in Berlin. He first came to prominence with his Einstein Tower observatory and laboratory in Potsdam (1921), a strongly phallic form which appeared to be made of concrete but was in fact rendered brick. Under the influence of the Dutch Expressionists, Mendelsohn turned to a quirky, angular geometric approach as in the Hat Factory at Luckenwalde (1923) but, with a

series of department stores in German cities, then developed his characteristic dynamic, streamlined urban style, with horizontal strips of metal windows and bands with rounded corners. In 1933, with the rise of Nazism, he emigrated to England and worked with Serge Chermayeff, notably on the De La Warr Pavilion at Bexhill-on-Sea (1935). In 1941, Mendelsohn went to live in San Francisco where he mainly designed buildings for the Jewish Community.

Mendelsohn rather resembled a tailor or bank manager in appearance, with round, thin-rimmed glasses, brushed back hair, prominent nose and ears, and a double chin. This *Archi-tête* has him as one of his early black Expressionist designs.

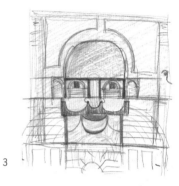

charles
moore

**charlie moore came to town,
riding on baloney,
laid a piazza down,
made of macaroni.**

Charles Moore (1925–1993), the Californian-based bad boy of Post-Modernism, spent the first twenty years of practice designing private houses (you could do that in California), typified by the Sea Ranch of 1965, 'a routine essay in redwood cabin regionalism'. His Kresge College, Santa Cruz (1974), with William Turnbull, took a combination of a Mediterranean village and Hadrian's Villa as model but treated it in a kitsch, pop art, eclectic, cardboard pastiche manner full of ironic 'anti-monuments'. It was derided by the students as 'Clown town' and as 'tacky pathos' by Charles Jencks. Moore's most famous work is the Piazza d'Italia fountain in New Orleans, which graced the cover of Jencks' *Language of Post-Modern Architecture* (1977). Ostensibly for the Italian community, it featured a contoured map of Italy surrounded by screens of a mish-mash of Classical orders, some composed of water jets or neon, and was full of jokey, ironic references (wetopes, deli orders, ironic capitals,

etc). It was to have been the centrepiece of a shopping precinct which never materialised. It was left isolated, rejected by the patronised community, vandalised and technically inept (the fountains never worked properly). Just like the old Modern Architecture it was supposed to supersede, in fact. Moore's legacy is a kind of stage-set, dissident frivolity which was a hallmark of much of the short-lived Post-Modern style in the US.

In appearance, Moore resembled a cherubic, avuncular, piscine, bald, inflated version of Edwin Lutyens, but pop-eyed behind large coloured-framed glasses. His sculptured metal face mask spits out water from one of the Piazza d'Italia arches, another 'double-coded' joke meaningless to non-architects. This *Archi-tête* presents Moore as an amalgam of the elements in the Piazza – paving, columns and porticos – together with the Hellman pun, 'Amoore Mio', loosely translated as 'I love me'.

Stage 1
1. Preliminary caricature from photographs

Stage 2
Study of building plans and architectural photographs
2. Piazza d'Italia, New Orleans

Stage 3
3. First freehand sketch

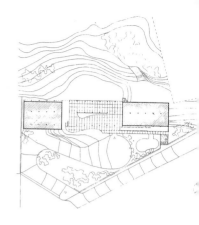

3.1

2

oscar
niemeyer

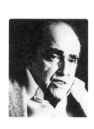

3.2

an architect returned from brasilia,
and said 'god, i've never felt sillier',
confused the great oscar
with lucio costa
and his manner could not have been chillier!

Stage 1
1. Preliminary caricature from photographs

Stage 2
Study of building plans and architectural photographs.
2. Grande Hotel 1940 Ouro Preto, Minas Gerais

Stage 3
3. First freehand sketches

Oscar Niemeyer (1907) is the foremost Brazilian architect and disciple of Le Corbusier with whom he worked on the Rio de Janiero Ministry of Education (1938). Niemeyer combined Corb's pre-war free plan, pilotis and white formalism with a freer, curvilinear, Spanish Colonial Baroque-influenced, 'stripped Gaudí' approach. Although a Marxist, he more often than not worked for the rich élite designing luxury houses, yacht clubs and casinos. His international fame blossomed when he designed all the main government buildings for Lúcio Costa's new capital Brasilia (1957–79). Like Chandigarh, Brasilia exhibits all the failures of megalomaniac new city planning, vast unused piazzas supporting shanty towns and cultural alienation. Somehow, Niemeyer's buildings express the division between the extreme poverty of the majority of Brazilians and the power and wealth of the rich, with their over-simplified monumentality, whimsy (upside down arches) and axial regimentation. Worst of all, like most air-conditioned glass slabs, they are inappropriate for the climate. Now in his nineties, Niemeyer has the appearance and gravitas of a carved Aztek patriarch. The *Archi-tête* relates to his Corb-inspired free-plan forms, (his own house, for example, or the early Pampúlha casino), with a swimming pool or Brasilia-style artificial lake for the body. He is surrounded by exotic landscaping, perhaps by Burle Marx with whom he worked and by whom he was inspired.

86

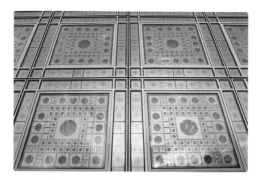

2

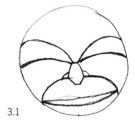

3.1

1

jean
nouvel

**i got a bell,
from jean nouvel,
he's drawn a mean
nouvel cuisine.**

3.2

Jean Nouvel (1945) is the most prolific and inventive of the 1968 generation of French architects, winning (and losing) more competitions than anyone else. He has been labelled High-Tech but this category is far too narrow to define his work which always stems from context, is conditioned by diurnal and seasonal change, makes play with shadow, light and transparency, is influenced by the post-Godard cinema (particularly Wenders) in terms of space and movement, incorporates industrial components *à la* Prouvé, yet may be influenced by traditional factors. *Les événéments de mai* made him aware of the political power of architecture and he has always sought to democratise space. At Nîmes he managed to increase the normal minimal sizes of social housing by 20 per

cent. His best-known building is the all-metal Insitut du Monde Arabe cultural centre in Paris (1987), one of Mitterrand's *grands projets*. Its main feature is the south wall in the form of a traditional Islamic *moucharabieh,* or pierced light-filtering gridded screen, which uses thirty thousand, state-of-the-(then)-art, camera-like, diaphragm apertures, controlled by photo-electric cells, which monitor the light and sun entering the building. Although costly, it does not really work but predicts future computer-controlled intelligent-building skin technology.

Nouvel looks like a French version of Yul Brynner: bald, intense, piercing eyes, sensuous mouth. The *Archi-tête* has him as a panel from the Arabe screen with a variety of facial expressions. *Un peu oriental?*

Hellman

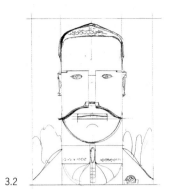

3.2

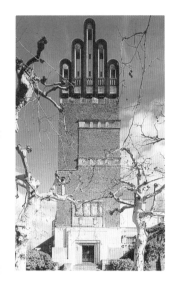

2

josef
olbrich

3.1

the secession in section,
reveals quite a confection,
or as described by some wit:
'gold sauerkraut, wiener schnitt.'

Joseph Maria Olbrich (1867–1908) was the third Austrian disciple of Otto Wagner to bridge the epochs from romantic to modern. If Loos was the Strauss of architecture, Olbrich was the Mahler, with his modern structures overlaid with symbolist detail. A founder member of the Wiener Secession, he designed its avant-garde, *Jugendstil* art gallery which was inspired by Klimt and topped with a dome of golden laurel leaves, the symbol of Parnassus, the victor's crown and the Apollonian muse. The Viennese immediately dubbed it The Golden Cabbage. Olbrich became architect to one of the aristocratic aesthetes of the time, the Grand Duke of Hesse, and designed his Darmstadt

complex of exhibition galleries and studios, notably the Ernst Ludwig (of Hesse) House with its Wagnerian/socialist realist statues, and the proto-Expressionist, five-finger-exercise wedding tower. Shades of Mendelsohn and Corb.

The young Olbrich cut rather a dashingly dapper figure, with the obligatory handle-bar moustache, wavy hair and intense gaze. The *Archi-tête* is composed from bits of his houses with windows for eyes, balustrades for ears, roofs for moustache and shoulders, and stained glass as tie. The hair is a version of his Darmstadt exhibition hall and the Secession building serves as a buttonhole. Spooky *Jugendstil* foliage forms the background.

Stage 2
Study of building plans and
architectural photographs
2. Hochzeitsturm

Stage 3
3. First freehand sketches

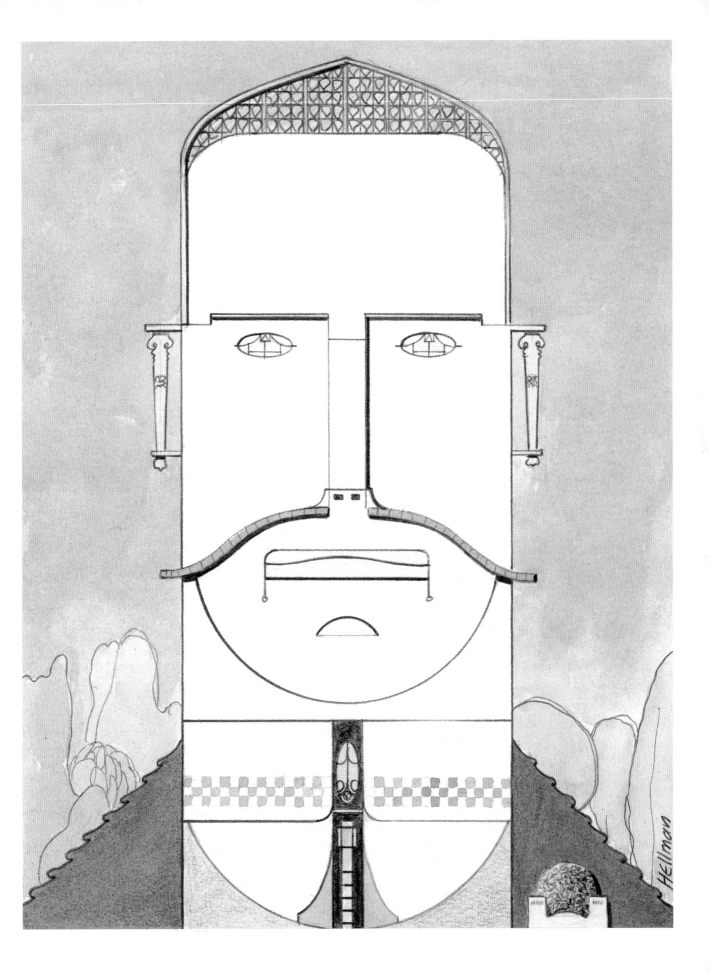

2

3

1

auguste perret

auguste perret made no apology,
for adopting rc technology,
(ideal for sensuous curves and dimples)
and forcing it into posts and lintels.

Stage 1
1. Preliminary caricature from photographs

Stage 2
Study of building plans and architectural photographs
2. Church at Le Raincy, France

Stage 3
3. First freehand sketch

Auguste Perret (1874–1954) was a French precursor of the Modern Movement, giving form and architectural coherence to reinforced concrete frame construction. The ingredients for his innovations were the structural engineering pioneers Viollet-le-Duc and Hennebique, Choisy and Guadet's theories of the structuralist essence of Classical and Gothic architecture, and his practical training as a builder in the family firm. His Paris flats in the rue Franklin (1905) expressed the framed construction (although tiled) with decorative infill panels and large windows, influencing Le Corbusier's *plan libre* approach, and the rue de Ponthieu garage (1902) left the painted concrete frame exposed. When Van de Velde called Perret in as concrete consultant for the Théâtre des Champs

Elysées, he soon found himself ousted as architect by Perret's superior technological expertise. The Church at Le Raincy (1923) uses slender, cylindrical columns and precast screens to give a vaguely Gothic effect. After the Second World War, Perret replanned Le Havre according to his concrete, stripped Neo-Classical principles, but the result is depressingly totalitarian in feel.

Perret's later appearance gives him the air of an old *roué*, with his straw *chapeau*, beard and curly moustache, boozer's nose, baggy eyes, cravat and spats. The *Archi-tête* combines the Le Havre reservoir for the hat, elements from Le Raincy for the face, beard and shoulders, and the Ponthieu garage window, suitably rendered as a *tricolore*, for the cravat. Perret style?

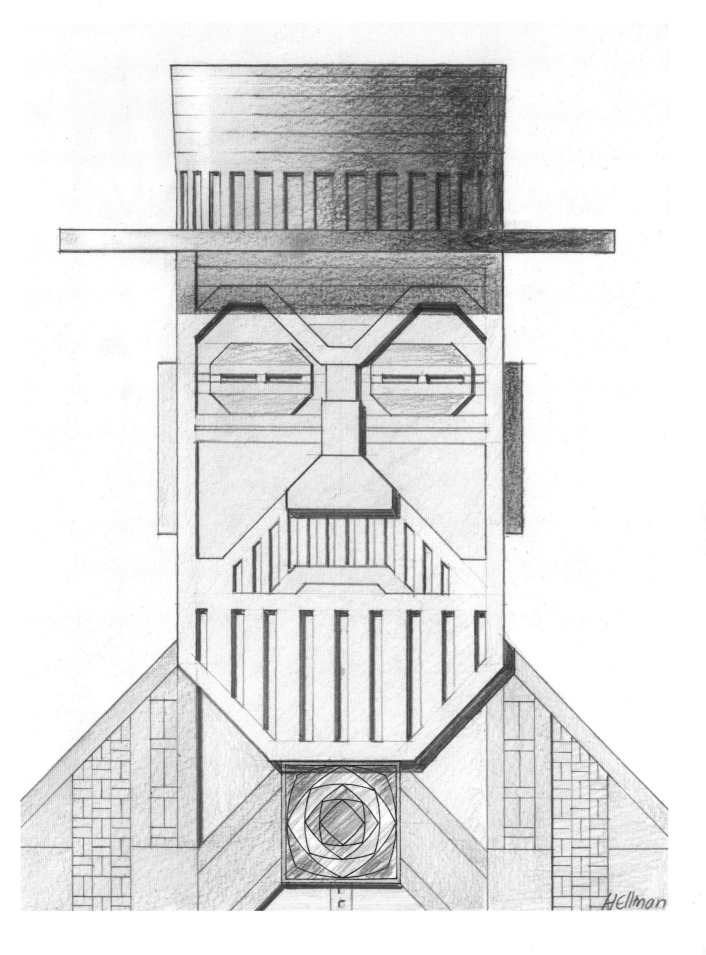

Hellman

3.1

2

1

renzo
piano

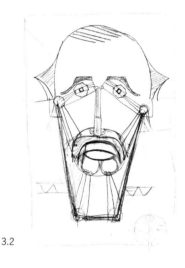
3.2

the pompidou centre for me,
is somewhere i do love to be,
because it's high-tech?
high-tech is it heck,
it's the one place in paris that's free!

Stage 1
1. Preliminary caricature from photographs

Stage 2
Study of building plans and architectural photographs
2. Menil Museum, Houston

Stage 3
3. First freehand sketches

Renzo Piano (1937), the multi-talented Genoese nominally High-Tech architect, first came to prominence when, in partnership with Richard Rogers, he designed the Pompidou arts centre in the old Les Halles quarter of Paris. To the lay world it was shockingly alien (dubbed the 'oil refinery' by Parisians) but in fact it trawled ideas from as far back as the Russian Revolution and Italian Futurism, as well as Archigram's 1960s space-age fantasies and crude notions of 'flexibility'. The free ride to the view from the top made the centre highly popular, but its inadequate detailing could not handle over twenty thousand visitors a day and massive renovation has had to be undertaken. Following the experience, Piano's work has sought to emphasise practicality, technological craftsmanship, a balance between science and

art, as well as anti-pomposity, non-'triumphalism' and encouragement of client participation, so long as the architect is the final arbiter. His Building Workshop in Genoa ranges from product, furniture, car and boat design to urban planning and mega buildings like the Osaka airport, which is fraught with technical problems to match its size.

Piano has something of the old hippie about him – long hair and beard, long face and sexy eyes – and he dresses in a tweedy *stile inglese*. The *Archi-tête* presents him as an engineering blueprint (by his structural engineer Peter Rice?) composed of parts of his buildings. Eyes and nose are fixings from the Navarra Research Centre, eyebrows are Menil Art Gallery light baffles, beard and hair are from the IBM 'Ladybird', and the jacket is part of the Menil front. *Piano nobile!*

1

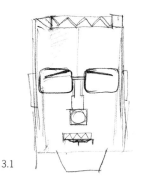

3.1

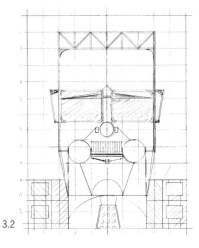

3.2

jean
prouvé

jean prouvé has still got the scars,
trying to make buildings like cars,
when he built one by the sorbonne,
he found that its big end had gone.

Jean Prouvé (1901–84) was the French grandfather of High-Tech, prefabrication and metal walling. Trained as an art metal worker in Nancy, he became involved in the production of architectural components through furniture design and in the 1930s pioneered light metal cladding, curtain walling, light-weight steel frames, space frames and tensile structures. His aims, in line with the Modern Movement, were to mass produce buildings like cars and to improve quality, cost and availability accordingly. Unfortunately, buildings, unlike cars, are multi-functional, static and long lasting and all-metal architecture requires continuous and expensive maintainence as Prouvé's heirs, Piano, Rogers, Foster and Nouvel, are still discovering.

Prouvé had the look of a typical French engineer: broom hair-cut, clipped moustache, wire-framed glasses. The *Archi-tête*, like that of Renzo Piano, has him as a blueprint with a light metal truss for hair, car-type windows as glasses, and pressed metal panels to form the body. *Allons enfants…*

Stage 1
1. Preliminary caricature from photographs

Stage 3
3.1 & 3.2 First freehand sketches

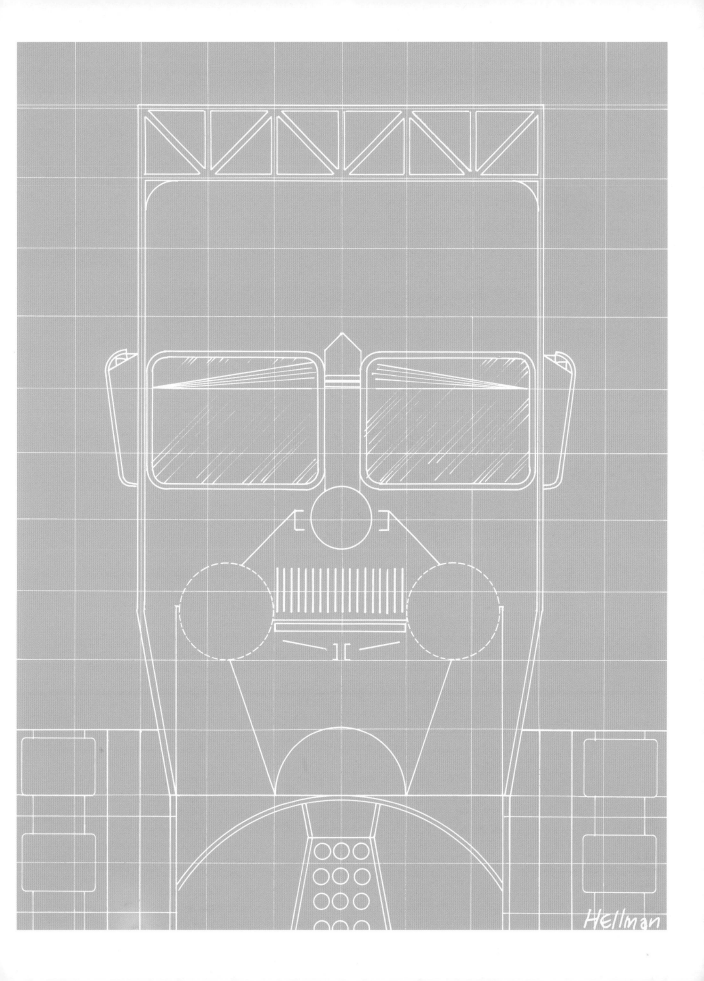

Hellman

richard rogers

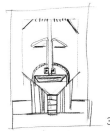

3

2

1

Stage 1
1. Preliminary caricature from photographs

Stage 2
Study of building plans and architectural photographs
2. Lloyds Building, London

Stage 3
3. First freehand sketch

Richard Rogers (1933) is, after Norman Foster, the most successful of the British High-Tech architects of the last quarter of the twentieth century. Born in Florence of Anglo-Italian bourgeois parents, Rogers met Foster at Yale where they came under the influence of Paul Rudolph, and later Buckminster Fuller and Louis Kahn, forming the short-lived Team 10 in London to pursue the application of advanced technology. In 1971, Rogers collaborated with Renzo Piano and won the Pompidou Centre competition with a design influenced by the space-age graphics of Archigram as well as pioneering the revival of pre-First World War Russian Constructivism and Italian Futurism. The Centre represents an obsessive celebration of the then current fashion for 'flexibility', with huge spans to provide structure, free floor areas, and services and stairs hung on the outside. In fact, this inhibited the use of the building which nevertheless proved to be more popular than the Eiffel Tower and Louvre together. In 1978, the 'left-wing' Rogers designed the all-steel Lloyds Insurance Company building in the City of London on the same

principles, putting lifts, toilets and services on the outside as functional decoration. Most employees dislike the building and its exterior requires constant maintenance, but it has become an icon in an area dominated by dull commercial boxes. As a dyslexic and a foreigner, Rogers was always the outsider. However, he is now very much part of the New Labour establishment being made first a knight, then a peer and now influencing government policy. Like many architects, his ideas are simplistic but his boyish enthusiasm to get things done against the odds is infectious.

In his sixties, Lord Rogers of Riverside (!) has the appearance of a balding Roman Emperor with aquiline nose and fleshy lips. He sports designer suits and shirts in clashing primary colours and refuses to wear a tie even in the House of Lords (quite a rebel). The *Archi-tête* (pre-Millennium Dome, sadly) has him as a version of the Lloyds Building with the arch form as head, ventilation ducting for nose and eyebrows, and escape stairs for ears. The body is in the style of the Pompidou Centre complete with *tricolore* vent shafts.

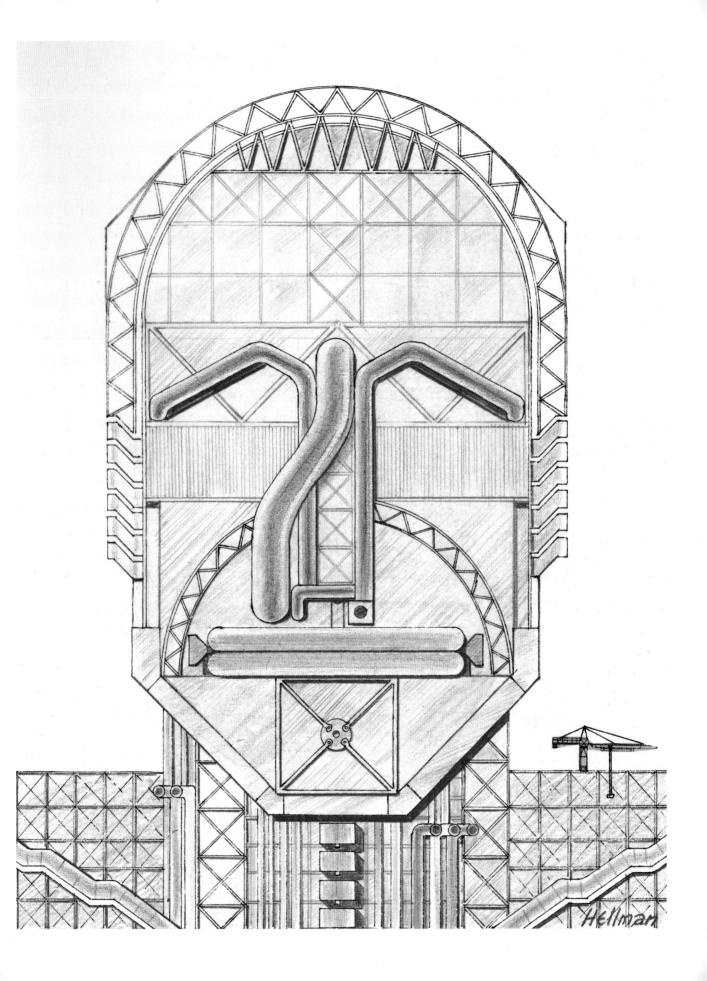

Hellman

2

3

aldo rossi

1

**aldo rossi was rational,
against styles international,
pursuing a different tack,
to turn the (alessi) clock back.**

Aldo Rossi (1931–98) was the leading Milanese theorist and practitioner of the Italian Post-Modern Neo-Rationalist school, *La Tendenza*. His 1966 publication *L'Architettura della Città* combined a critique of destructive Modern Movement town planning in old cities with an attempt to codify an inventory of eternal building prototypes. These were based on the nineteenth-century, stripped geometric Neo-Classicism of Boullée and Ledoux, as well as Adolf Loos' theories, vernacular structures and De Chirico's surrealist images of fear and foreboding in the piazza. Rossi was opposed to Functionalism and subservience to the brief or consumerism, proposing instead universal building types which employed a limited range of forms – squares, polygons and cylinders. These were to be autonomous; changing functions were to adapt to them, not vice versa. Unfortunately, Rossi's buildings tend to evoke coldness, foreboding or monotony. They are also technically inept, as his 1973

Gallaratese housing shows, a case of too much intellectual theorising and not enough intuitive practice. This is fine for mausoleums or cemeteries, but verges on the ludicrous when applied to commercial ventures such as Alessi products or the Il Palazzo hotel in Japan – though they will make fine decomposed ruins in the not-too-distant future.

Rossi was described as having great charm and a child-like innocence, essential qualities for a Rationalist. In photographs, he appears rather sad and apprehensive, with 'oyster' eyes, bent nose and sprouting hair. The *Archi-tête*, painted his favourite terracotta, rationalises him *à la* the Modena cemetery on fat Gallaratese pilotis with concentric circles for eyes – although he does not seem to have used circles (artist's license). His tie is a version of the floating *Teatro del Mondo* for the 1980 Venice Biennale, one of his more sympathetic designs, while his shoulders are based on Il Palazzo.

Hellman

1

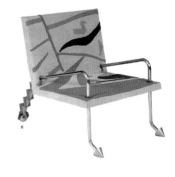

2

3

ettore
sottsass

furniture seen through memphis' eyes, only serves to emphasise, chairs built to shock and not to last, will land you flat on your sottsass.

Stage 1
1. Preliminary caricature from photographs

Stage 2
Study of building plans and architectural photographs
2. A witty answer to the puritanical and perfect structure of Bauhaus chairs

Stage 3
3. First freehand sketch

Ettore Sottsass is the architect, leading light, of the Milanese Memphis group of designers who caused a sensation at the 1981 Milan Furniture Fair with their ultra Post-Modern artefacts. Self-styled as the 'post-radical avant-garde', Memphis deliberately reacted to Modern Movement puritanical Functionalism and the industrial 'good taste' aesthetic. They sought inspiration in the kitsch and the 'banal' world of science-fiction comics, pop art, Disney and commercial advertising, with a dose of Art Deco. They revived pattern and decoration while juxtaposing modern and traditional materials such as laminates, textured metal sheet, celluloids, printed glass, fireflake finishes, industrial paints, neon, marble and hardwoods in irrational shapes. The range extended to furniture, lamps, ceramics, glass and laminates, but not buildings, although Graves and Isozaki were on their wavelength and designed pieces for them. The name Memphis was supposedly inspired by the Bob Dylan song *Stuck inside of Mobile with the Memphis blues again,* with particular reference to the final lines, 'Your debutante just knows what you need, but I know what you want,' a neat reversal of the old Modernist dictum. (Incidentally, 'mobile' is Italian for furniture.)

The fashion for Memphis was short-lived, and despite the rhetoric, its expensive one-off products were often just badly designed and silly, suitable for rich fashion designers and pop stars rather than the mass market. If your aspiration is Micky Mouse you get Goofy.

Sottsass has a lugubriously mournful air, droopy moustache and heavy-lidded eyes. The *Archi-tête* turns him into one of Memphis' unusable lamps with variations on their 'bacteria' laminates for hair, twisted table leg for the nose, combined hardwood and plastic furniture as moustache and various assorted liquorice sweet-inspired elements for eyes, eyebrows and ears. *La donna è mobile!*

Hellman

philippe starck

a french person called philippe starck,
did all his designs in the darck,
he would toss off a stool,
in the form of a tool,
or a building that looked like a sharck.

1

2

3.1

3.2

Stage 1
1. Preliminary caricature from photographs

Stage 2
Study of building plans and architectural photographs
2. Flamme d'Or beer hall, Tokyo

Stage 3
3. First freehand sketches

Philippe Starck (1949), son of a French aeronautics engineer, is the wild man of design. Anarchic, energetic and endlessly inventive, he can turn his hand to anything from a toothbrush to an office block with imagination, wit and technical expertise. Like Jean Nouvel, Starck's ideology was forged in the heat of the 1968 Paris student uprising and he draws on influences outside the traditional confines of product design including cinema, the sci-fi novels of Philip K Dick of *Bladerunner* fame (Starck named his chairs after the stories' characters), literature, painting and mythology. By 1968, Starck had his own company designing inflatables; in the 1970s, he did the interiors for two nightclubs; and in 1982, President Mitterand notoriously commissioned him to revamp part of the Elysées Palace, incorporating the satirical Richard III chair, bourgeois at the front, empty behind. In the late 1980s Starck designed the interior of New York's Royalton Hotel, full of Post-Modern symbolism, and whole buildings in Japan. Here his lack of architectural inhibitions resulted in wonderfully over-the-top shapes with names like *Nani Nani* (The Un-nameable), a biomorphic Godzilla-like building clad in oxidised copper,

Le Baron Vert based on Fontana's slash paintings and *La Flamme* for Ashai Beer, a swaying black box topped with an erotic gold flame. Starck's techno/existential, metaphor-as-message approach may verge on the self-indulgent but he usually avoids the whimsical silliness of much Post-Modernism. His motto (after Wilde) is: 'Feet in the gutter, head in the stars.'

Starck's appearance fits with his energetic, outsider stance. With his freaked-out Eraserhead haircut, gimlet eyes, pear-shaped face and designer stubble, he roars through cities on the Starckmobile motorbike designed by himself, of course. The *Archi-tête* uses the *Mister Meumeu* Parmisan cheese dish like one of Starck's comic hats; the hair is a variation on the *La Flamme* finial; the eyebrows are a Fluocaril toothbrush and an Apriti lever handle; the nose is a toilet brush holder; the eyes are a refuse bin and vent outlet; the mouth is a coffee table; the moustache a chair; and the beard is an inverted spider-form *Juicy Salif* lemon squeezer. The collar and shirt are based on the *Boom Rang* chair and the shoulders the *Baron Vert* and *Nani Nani* buildings. Starck raving mad!

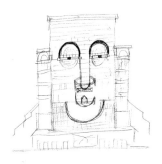

3

1

2

james
stirling

big jim had a stirling crisis,
't was by the cam, not the isis,
where he had quite a nasty turn,
called post-modern change of heart burn.

Stage 1
1. Preliminary caricature from
photographs

Stage 2
Study of building plans and
architectural photographs
2. Neue Staatsgalerie, Stuttgart

Stage 3
3. First freehand sketch

James Stirling (1926–92) was one of the Big Three post-war British architects. The son of a Glasgow marine engineer, he studied at Liverpool University and in 1956 he set up a London practice with James Gowan. Stirling was like a sponge, absorbing every kind of style and influence, new or old. The Leicester University Engineering Building (1963) in concrete, red glazed tiling and patent glazing changed the course of British architecture and patent glazing shares. In it, critics traced aspects of Northern vernacular, Telford, Butterfield, Le Corbusier, Futurism, Russian Constructivism, Meyer, Wright , Kahn etc (phew!). After the split with Gowan, Stirling pursued the tile/glazing mode in the Cambridge History Library (1967) and the Florey student hostel in Oxford (1971) both formal *tours de force* but still Modernist, especially in the fact that they leaked and had intolerable internal environments.

A fundamental stripey-stone-monumental-with-High-Tech-collaged-bits change of direction came with the Staatsgalerie, Stuttgart (1984), but now the influences were the current Post-Modern ones of Hadrian's Villa, Ledoux and Schinkel. Two buildings in London, the Tate Gallery extension (1987) and the No 1 Poultry office block, continue this style which seems to have degenerated into inflated Toy Town neo-Noddy. Unhappily, Stirling's untimely end confirmed the old
sick joke that architects build their mistakes while doctors bury theirs.

'Big Jim' was literally a great figure to caricature, elephantine, fleshy, huge-nosed, piggy- eyed, double chinned, he always wore blue shirts. Such details are a gift to cartooning.The *Archi-tête* has Jim as a Stuttgart-style rotunda with stripey Neo-Classical ears and bits of Cambridge tile, glass and tube for jacket and tie. Jimbo!

Hellman

1

2

3

bernard
tschumi

bernard tschumi, looking gloomy, said, 'i need a large derrida!'

Stage 1
1. Preliminary caricature from photographs

Stage 2
Study of building plans and architectural photographs
2. Folies in the Parc de la Villette, Paris

Stage 3
3. First freehand sketch

Bernard Tschumi (1944), Swiss born but practising in Paris and New York, is one of the leading exponents of French Deconstructivism, part of the post-1968 generation, like Nouvel and Koolhaas, who reacted against Post-Modernism. For ten years after qualifying, Tschumi taught in London and New York while developing theoretical notions on the influence of other media on architecture such as cinema, painting, literature and literary philosophy, especially Derrida. He set up office in 1981 and immediately won the major competition to masterplan the Parc la Villette (1982–95) on a vast, defunct industrial site in northern Paris, one of President Mitterrand's *grands projets*. Tschumi's design imposed an ordering grid over the site with the intersections marked by red painted-steel *folies*, some sculptural, some

functional, derived from Russian constructivists like Chernikhov and El Lissitsky as well as Eisenman, and a linking covered way. Amongst these are buildings by Nouvel and De Portzamparc, a slaughterhouse converted into a science museum, sunken sound gardens, children's play areas, canals and bridges and so on. Despite difficulties due to changes of government, this hugely popular urban park demonstrates the power of the French state to get things done and patronise avant-garde ideas.

Tschumi has a rather ruggedly handsome, male model appearance, with full lips, greying temples and a firm dimpled chin. The *Archi-tête* naturally portrays him as a version of one of his Villette pavilions, with a perforated balustrade as scarf. *Folie de grandeur*.

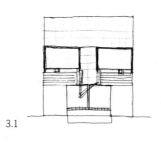

3.1

3.2

ludwig
mies van der rohe

herr ludwig mies van der rohe,
detailed the seagram in one go,
on two a4 sheets if you please,
as he said, 'less drawings, more fees!'

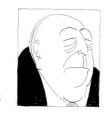

1

Stage 1
1. Preliminary caricature from photographs

Stage 2
Study of building plans and architectural photographs
2. Office tower in Baltimore

Stage 3
3.1 & 3.2 First freehand sketches

Ludwig Mies van der Rohe (1886–1969), known to architects simply as Mies, was one of the great German pioneers of the Modern Movement. He expropriated the epithet 'Less is more, almost nothing' from Eastern philosophy to define his minimalist approach to design. This combined mass-produced repetition, Neo-Classical austerity and Japanese simplicity to evolve a universal building type consisting of steel-framed structures with glass or brick infill. Refinement, quality and craft were essential ingredients, as summed up in Mies' dictum, 'God is in the details' ('But get it in writing,' Sam Goldwyn might have added).

He helped to invent modern architecture in Germany and took over the Bauhaus in 1930 – though it was later closed by the Nazis (with whom it has been said he collaborated). He then moved to the USA to apply his method to universities, expensive housing or temples of high consumerism such as that bronze monument to whisky, the Seagram Building in New York. However, the line between simplicity and sterility is a fine one, and each of Mies' buildings, whether a boiler house or church, tends to look the same. Mies represented everything that was wrong with modern architecture to the Post-Modernists like Venturi, who satirised his catch phrase into 'Less is a bore' (ho ho), but his reputation has already outshone that short-lived movement.

Mies' appearance seems always to have resembled a portly, heavy-jowled, affable Ruhr industrialist or politician, invariably fingering an expensive, king-sized, full corona Havana cigar. The *Archi-tête* shows him as one of his typical symmetrical, axial plans, conforming to a strict grid and in which nothing is out of line.

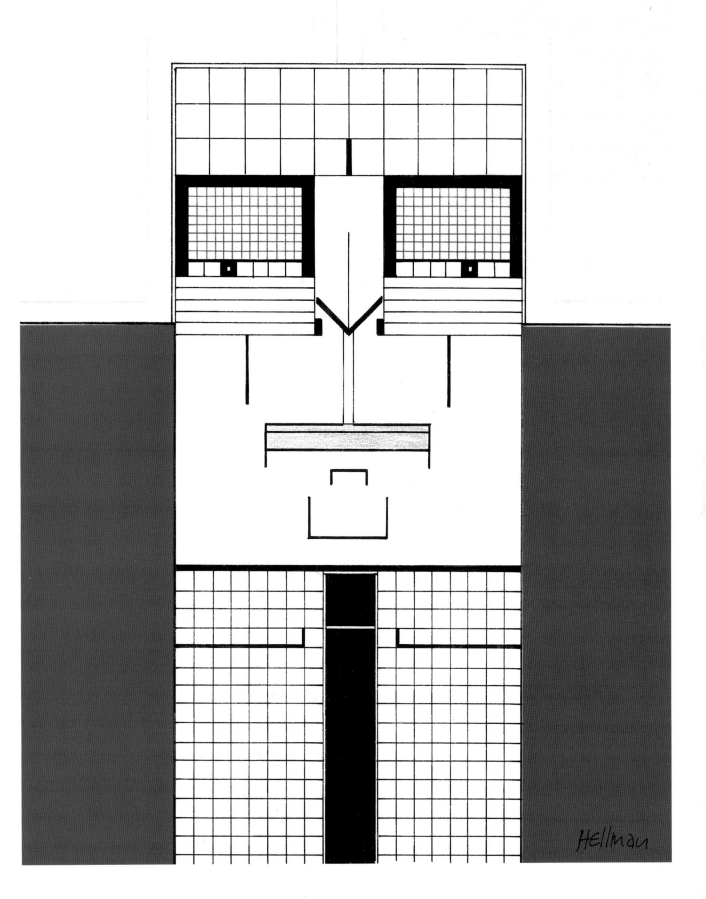

Hellman

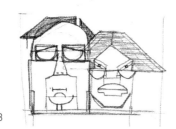

3

2

venturi
scott brown

the venturis in rose-tinted specs, travelled all around vegas with decks of cards which were marked and then they embarked on tricks contradictory and complex.

Stage 1
1. Preliminary caricature from photographs

Stage 2
Study of building plans and architectural photographs
2. Gordon Wu Hall, Princeton

Stage 3
3. First freehand sketch

Robert Venturi (1925), with his wife and architect partner Denise Scott Brown (1931), is the American prophet of Post-Modernism with two polemical tracts riding on the growing 1960s disillusionment with Modern Movement reductivism. *Complexity and Contradiction in Architecture* (1966) argued for a return to commonly understood meaning and symbolism based on historical and vernacular precedent. In *Learning From Las Vegas* (1972) the Venturis analysed the city and discerned a truly American, popular, anti-art culture, while omitting to mention that it was run by gangsters, pimps and drug barons, and was polluting the Nevada desert. In effect, they opened a Pandora's box return to pastiche and eclecticism denying any political or social context to architectural design which was seen purely as a matter of aesthetics and style. Charles Jencks, in his influential *The Language of Post-Modern Architecture* (1977) which commandeered the term Post-Modernism from literary criticism, narrowly defined architecture as language with grammar and syntax, giving authenticity to the

Venturi's call for a return to familiar or ironic signs and symbols. Post-Modernism became the ideal style of 'Marketecture' for the Reagan/Thatcher *laissez-faire* 1980s, unleashing a flood of sterile commercial blocks adorned with cardboard pediments and columns. Unhappily, the Venturis are rather second-rate architects, self-consciously translating their new dogmas into built form while deflecting any criticism by maintaining that any bad aspects are deliberate or 'ironic'. Clever, it must be said.

The original *Archi-tête* of Robert Venturi in the mid-1980s portrayed him in a younger, somewhat simian incarnation as a version of the house he designed for mom, with a Vegas-style billboard and cars on the Strip. The revised version gives the somewhat school marm-like Scott Brown her proper place under Venturi, again as a house reminiscent of the Colorado timber dwelling, with a piece of the Princetown College marble for Venturi's nose. The whole is crowned by a Guild House-style TV aerial, a suitable 'double-coded' symbol for an aged couple.

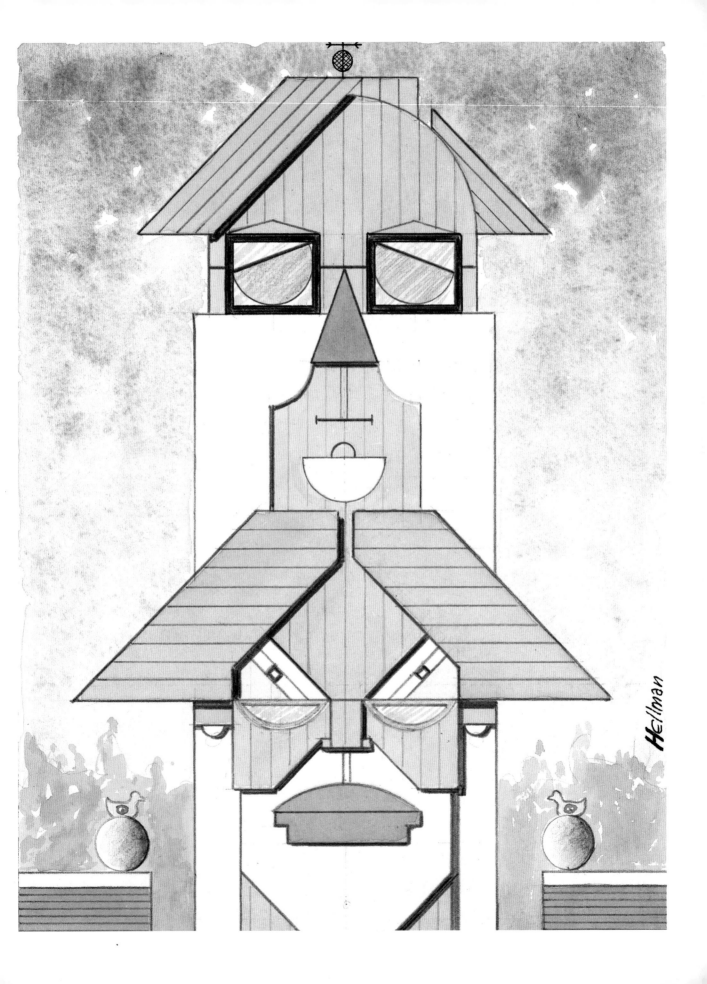

2

3.1

3.2

charles
voysey

the houses of cfa voysey,
could not be thought loud, brash or noisy,
their colours are chaste,
applied with good taste,
in green, white and black, not cramoisey.

Stage 1
1. Preliminary caricature from photographs

Stage 2
Study of building plans and architectural photographs.
2. Broadleys, near Windermere, Westmorland. Perspective of the terrace front with inset plans, 1898

Stage 3
3. First freehand sketches

Charles Francis Annesley Voysey (1857–1941), like Mackintosh, combined the approach of the Arts and Crafts movement, initiated by William Morris, and Art Nouveau. His work was mainly in the domestic field and purported to draw on local English traditions, but in effect he developed a personal 'vernacular' style consisting of white rendered walls, pitched slate roofs and black iron windows and trimmings, whether in the Lake District or Bedford Park. The Art Nouveau style was employed in the joinery or metalwork details, particularly the heart motif. Voysey was highly principled and would not work for clients he felt did not believe wholeheartedly in his philosophy. Consequently, when the Arts and Crafts style became unfashionable after the

war, his commissions dried up and he had to resort to wallpaper and tile designing. His functional, simplified buildings were thought to be precursors of the Modern Movement which he despised. Nevertheless, his architecture was successful, enduring and popular since it influenced thousands of spec-built, suburban, semi-dets from the 1930s onwards.

Voysey's thin, bony ascetic appearance gave him the air of a Victorian parson or undertaker. He designed his own clothes according to strictly functional principles, doing away with lapels as unnecessary, for example. This *Archi-tête* was inspired by Voysey's brilliantly executed watercolour renderings of his designs, particularly Broadleys, Windermere (1899) with its banks of sunflowers.

114

Hellman

2

1

3.1

otto
wagner

3.2

otto wagner could not have been bluer,
when approached by a fan from the ruhr,
who said 'i love your stuff,
i just can't get enough
could you hum a bit from your die valkure?'

Otto Wagner (1841–1918), the Austrian prophet of the Modern Movement, founded the Vienna School with his disciples Hoffmann, Olbrich and Loos (not to be confused with the firm of solicitors). Wagner started as a neo-Schinkel Classicist, moved to a geometric version of Art Nouveau and finally to a proto-Functionalism/Rationalism in line with Austro-Hungarian state republican benevolence, proclaiming that architecture should tackle the problems of the real world using modern technology. For some reason, this translated into horizontal lines and flat roofs, and the misplaced Platonic philosophy that 'Nothing that is not useful can be beautiful.' This did not stop him putting 'useless' winged victories on top of his famous 1906 Post Office Savings Bank in Vienna (symbols of first-class post?) with its very modern top-lit banking hall and boldly exposed aluminium fixings to its marbled cladding – but what architects do and say are very different matters.

Wagner's appearance in later life was avuncular and professorial, with his curly white beard and moustachio, pince-nez glasses and balding pate, a bit like Emil Jannings in *The Blue Angel*. The *Archi-tête* combines the first design for the Savings Bank (spectacles and hair) with the golden dome of the church at Steinhoff (head), a version of the winged victories (nose and moustache), a *Jugendstil* capital (mouth) and marble bolt-on cladding (shirt). *Götterdammerung!*

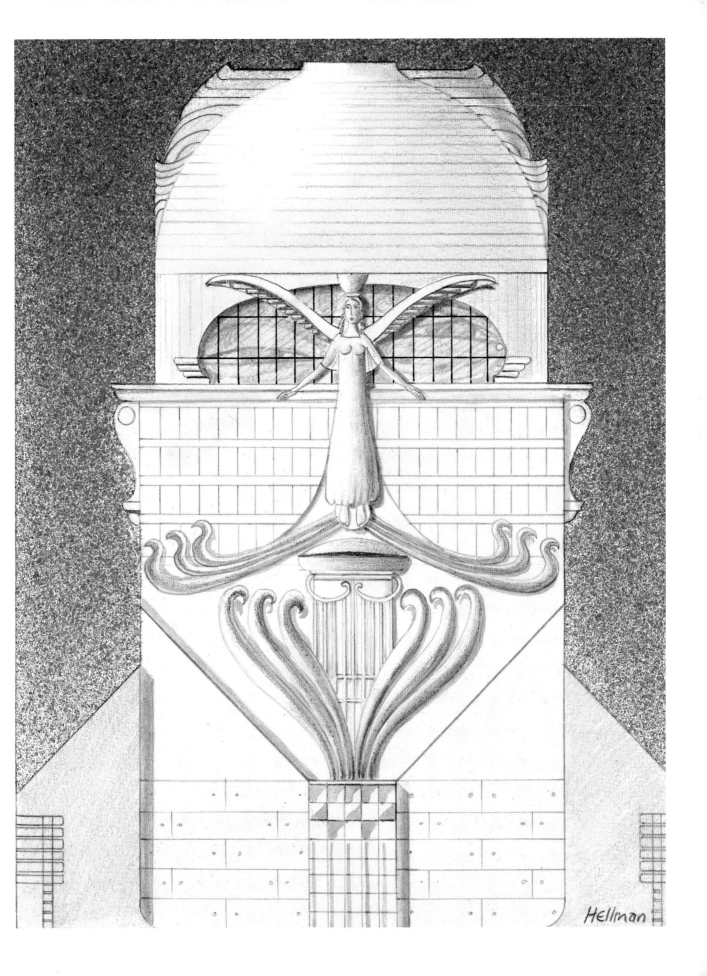

Hellman

3

2

1

frank lloyd
wright

frank lloyd wright, while working in plains,
said 'now if my client complains
that his organic roof,
isn't quite waterproof,
i say "well move your chair when it rains!"'

Stage 1
1. Preliminary caricature from photographs

Stage 2
Study of building plans and architectural photographs
2. Falling Water, Bear Run, Pennsylvania

Stage 3
3. First freehand sketch

Frank Lloyd Wright (1867–1959) was the greatest 20th-century American architect, creating during a 70-year career some of the masterpieces of modern architecture. His roots were in the 19th-century American individualism of Whitman, Thoreau and Emerson and the English Arts and Crafts movement also influenced by Sullivan, the traditional Japanese house and native American culture, he developed his philosophy of organic architecture at one with nature and drawing inspiration from its forms. A great self publicist, Wright feigned opposition to the European Modern Movement while at the same time influencing it and pioneering the use of advanced technology. His Utopian and paternalist town planning ideas were the opposite of urbanists like Le Corbusier, involving self-sufficient, low-rise garden cities, which at the end of the century arè being seriously considered as a sustainable alternative.

Wright cultivated a deliberately eccentric image, part 19th-century romantic artist, part mid-Western land owner. He was described by Alistair Cooke in an obituary as resembling

'Merlin posing as Whistler's mother. Indeed, there was always a curiously feminine grace about him. He looked . . . like the matriarch of a pioneer family.' The aged Wright also had a touch of Harpo Marx, Bertrand Russell and Quentin Crisp about him. He sported longish hair, tweed cloaks made by up-market Chicago tailors, flowing cravats or string ties, wide-brimmed western-style hats or large berets, breeches, laced-up boots or brogues and a malacca walking cane but, typically, he drove a state-of-the-art red Lincoln Zephyr.

This *Archi-tête*, exaggerates and extends the hat brim to resemble one of the master's long prairie house roof cantilevers, as exemplified in the 1909 Robie House, Chigago, growing out of the rocky hillside which symbolises the cape. The facial caricature is based on a typical Art Deco Wright stained glass window design, while the tie is a waterfall reference to the 1936 Kaufmann House known as 'Falling Water'. The clasped hands, a device Wright used to demonstrate the principles of organic structures in tension, might be one of his native American inspired churches. Wright is might!

Hellman

tony blair

2

tony blair,
teeth and hair,
manic stare,
thatcher's heir?

1

Tony Blair (1953) won the 1997 election for Labour, sweeping aside eighteen years of Conservative rule with a huge majority. At the same time, he swept away a hundred years of Labour/socialist ideals from Clause 4 to the right to strike, from the hegemony of the working class to the untouchability of the Welfare State. This change of direction was brand-imaged as New Labour or the Third Way, implying a compromise between 'Old Labour' collectivist dogma and Tory self-interest. In effect, Blair has carried on much of Thatcher's monetarist 'revolution', realising that to win elections he should borrow policies that seemed popular, especially to the new property-owning, car-running, middle-management middle classes. The poor, underprivileged or unemployed did not vote anyway, and as far as Old Labour's traditional support, the industrial working class, went, well, by previous definitions there were few remaining. In the face of the huge majority, how could Old Labour raise any objection? Blair has even adopted Thatcher's election-winning involvement in a 'just war' in the Balkans, operating as America's sub-contractor in NATO and being photographed smiling in various war machines.

Architecturally this seamless continuity is symbolised by the Millennium Dome designed by Labour Peer Lord Rogers of Riverdance which was taken over from the Conservatives. This incredibly expensive (the cost could be over a billion pounds, though they probably won't tell us that) tent is a fine monument to New Labour: temporary and mis-named (not a 'dome' but a tensile structure). On the surface, Blair seems to have reversed the philistinism of Thatcher by proclaiming support for the arts and 'culture', but in fact continues to cut grants and rely on the Lottery. In architecture, he has set up a Commission for Architecture and the Built Environment, headed by property speculator Stuart Lipton, but at the same time continues the Conservative's Private Finance Initiative whereby private developers build and lease to the public sector, the proposed new London Assembly building being a prime example.

Cartoonists quickly identified 'President' Blair's characteristics as all ears and teeth, with manic eyes, protruding lower lip and receding hair. Of course, he does not really look like this, but caricature is not about representation and it sums up his rather earnest, grinning disposition. The *Archi-tête* draws on these exaggerations to make him into a New Labour HQ, approached by the Third Way and flanked by obsolete Old Labour Modernism and Conservative Neo-Classicism.

Stage 1
1. Preliminary caricature from photographs

Stage 2
Study of building plans and architectural photographs
2. Millennium Dome, London

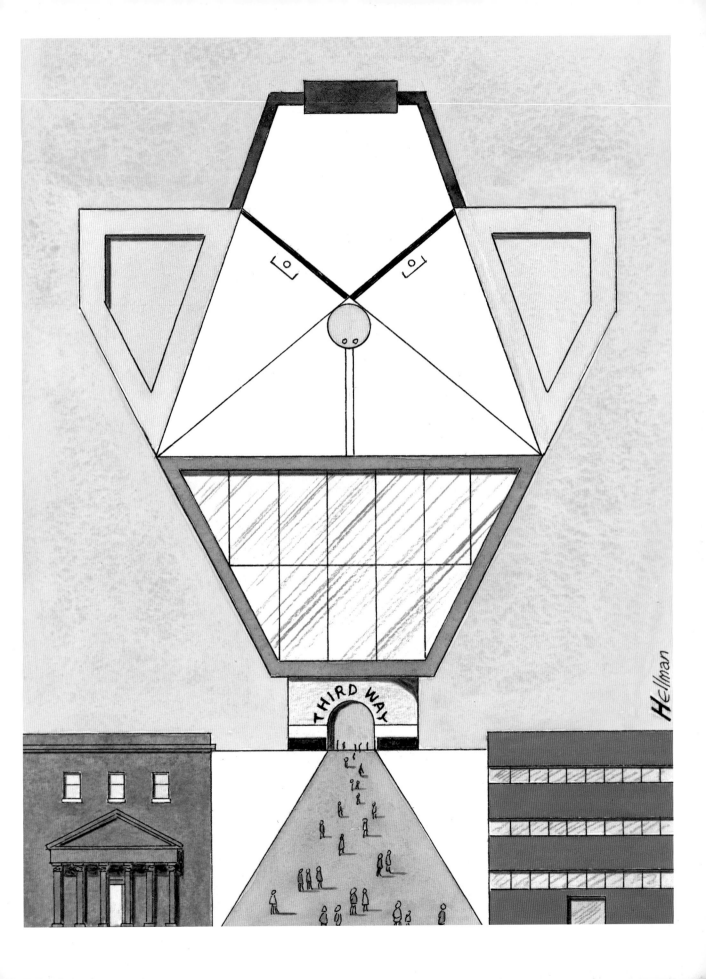

THIRD WAY

Hellman

prince charles

prince charles' appearance,
lacks formal coherence,
like a taxi with jaws,
and two wide-open doors.

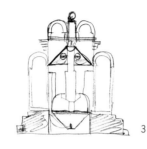
3

2

1

Stage 1
1. Preliminary caricature from photographs

Stage 2
Study of building plans and architectural photographs
2. Poundbury, Dorset

Stage 3
3. First freehand sketch

The Prince of Wales through history has appeared the more parasitic member of the Royal family, just waiting for a parent to snuff it, and by the 1980s there were constant mutterings that Charles (1948) should get a proper job. It must have been suggested that some innocuous interest or hobby like architecture or the environment would help fill the void and give him something to do. Charles' views on architecture first resounded like a dropped brick in 1984 when he was asked to address the RIBA centenary bash at Hampton Court. Instead of mouthing the usual anodyne platitudes, Charles launched an attack on modern architecture specifically bad-mouthing two London projects which were the subject of planning applications, No1 Poultry and the National Gallery extension. The first he likened to a 'stump' and the second to a 'carbuncle', the first of many seat-of-the-pants aesthetic epithets to come. Of course architecture, particularly large schemes, is not just a matter of aesthetic preference but a political act. Could Charles have been so naïve as not to realise that his interventions were political and legal, interfering in the democratic planning process? As a result, both Modernist schemes were rejected and replaced by excruciating Post-Modern-Classical blocks.

Charles' architectural advisers probably suggested he put forward some positive alternative suggestions to his stylistic condemnations. These turned out to be something vaguely called Community Architecture, which had been around for

decades under various names like 'participation' or consulting 'the people', and an equally vague return to decoration and meaning which Post-Modernists had been advocating since the mid-1960s. Charles also published his own architectural magazine *Perspectives*, set up his own architecture school and, with Leon Krier, built his own out-of-town model development on his land at Poundbury in Dorset. All three have been unmitigating disasters. Charles could have confined himself to intelligent comment and erudite analysis but these would not have made the headlines. Charles' 'sight-bite' name calling epitomises his generation of royals' desire for publicity and it has invariably back-fired. Charles has lost the battle to return to some mythical golden age where communities of forelock-touching plebs were at one with their buildings. All his interventions have resulted in is an even greater loss of planning nerve as supermarkets are dressed up as rustic barns and everything new must be 'in keeping' with the surrounding mediocrity. The hated Modernists like Rogers, Foster and Hopkins are now the be-knighted establishment. Poor old Charlie.

With Charles and Thatcher, the 1980s were a great time for cartoonists. Charles is a god-send for caricaturists, with his huge ears, long nose, piggy eyes and visage that looks like it has been crudely cobbled together from two quite different faces. The *Archi-tête* has him as a decaying Classical monument that has long outlasted its relevance.

Hellman

ronald
reagan

ronald reagan at seventy-six,
exploited all his old show-biz tricks,
his hair and make-up were from the start,
'a triumph of the embalmer's art.' (gore vidal)

3

1

Stage 1
1. Preliminary caricature from photographs

Stage 3
3. First freehand sketch

Ronald Reagan (1911) as an ex-Hollywood B-movie actor (*Bedtime With Bozo* was his crowning achievement) perfected a deliberately laconic, affably bumbling, absent-minded style which made him popular with Middle America. He won the Republican nomination and became President in 1980 and was re-elected for a second term in 1984. His air of disinterested detachment enabled him to survive an assassination attempt, wriggle out of any liability for the Iran-Contra scandal, and avoid responsibility for the economic disasters resulting from his policies. It was widely known that his wife Nancy, also a second-rate-movie actress but wealthy, wore the trousers and dictated many of Reagan's right-wing policies such as tax cuts for the rich, reductions to the welfare programme and massive defence expenditure.

Reagan's reign paralleled that of Mrs Thatcher who took the 'special relationship' to new heights of sycophancy. Both came to power by defeating discredited left/liberals (Callaghan and Carter), both adopted dogmatic monetarist policies and both waged war on weak countries (Argentina and Grenada) to whip up xenophobic support. Reagan was lucky enough to be President when the USSR and its 'evil empire' started

to crumble, having high-level meetings on *détente* initiated by Gorbachev which ended in the 1987 scrapping of intermediate nuclear forces treaty. This did not stop Reagan developing the Star Wars programme which finally put an end to the USSR's world power status: it just could not afford to keep up with the nuclear race, making Reagan appear both peace-maker and Cold War victor. However, the West's refusal, dominated by the US, to assist Gorbachev's reforms with economic aid led to his downfall and the economic, political and social crisis that exists in Russia today.

Reagan does not seem to have had any interest in architecture; but, as in Britain, Post-Modernism was the appropriate style for the 1980s, conservative, commercial, anti-liberal/Modernist, bombastic, superficial and mock-traditional. Graves, Johnson, Venturi and Moore might be said to typify the Reagan years, pseudo-radicalism with an arguable level of any moral or social awareness.

'Hopalong' Reagan was good to caricature with his dyed, quiffed-up hair, quizzical blank expression and grease paint-ravaged face. The *Archi-tête* presents him as a Post-Modern mid-western dwelling, clad in clapped-out boarding.

margaret
thatcher

what's horrible to work with, has a tendency to scratch, and rots after some ten years? i refer, of course, to thatch!

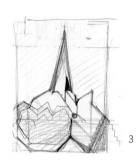

Margaret Thatcher (1925) was the Ironic Lady. She became Britain's first woman Prime Minister in 1979 yet was a anti-feminist. She promised to bring 'harmony' but introduced an era of division, strikes and protest. She promised to loosen 'state control' yet passed more restrictive legislation than any previous government. She extolled 'democracy' but emasculated the unions and local councils and abolished London's elected authority. She preached sensible, home-based economics yet sold off most of the country's assets in a bid for privatisation which benefited her wealthy supporters. She ostensibly upheld 'family values' yet destroyed Britain's manufacturing base, causing mass unemployment, homelessness and increased domestic crime. She lauded 'Britishness' and 'Victorian values' but exemplified its worst aspects. Needless to say, she won three elections and reigned for an unprecedented eleven years. In the end she believed in the myth of her own invincibility and became a liability which the Tories swiftly disposed of, installing what they (mistakenly) believed to be her antidote, the grey, boring, working-class John Major. Post-Modernism was the appropriate style for the Thatcher 1980s,

essentially conventional modern structures dressed up with stuck-on cardboard mock-Classical elements in an attempt to make them 'popular'. Thatcher seemed to hate the professions and was opposed to planning, and the architectural legacy of her premiership lay in suburban supermarkets pretending to be rural barns, 'yuppie' housing in converted sold-off council houses and Canary Wharf, a monument to ruthless *laissez-faire* gigantism (though with a three-billion pound plus public subsidy 'incentive'). During 1979–91 most public-sector architecture such as housing, schools or hospitals was abandoned for these actions we are now paying for.

Margaret Thatcher's somewhat artificially manufactured image was established soon after her rise to power, Bride-of-Frankenstein hair, manic stare, razor nose, prehensile mouth, blue dress, pearls and handbag. Political cartoonists initially had problems with her, being mostly male and not used to caricaturing women, until Steve Bell created the image of her as stark raving bonkers. The *Archi-tête* has her as a soon-to-rust iron monument. The lady must be turned to get the likeness.

Stage 1
1. Preliminary caricature from photographs

Stage 2
Study of building plans and architectural photographs
2. Canary Wharf, London

Stage 3
3. First freehand sketch